Oxford AQA GCSE History

America 1840-1895

Expansion and Consolidation

Revision Guide

 RECAP    APPLY   REVIEW    SUCCEED

Changes to the AQA GCSE History specification 8145 (Version 1.3) and support for these changes

AQA released Version 1.3 of their AQA GCSE History specification in September 2019. The changes are to the command words and stems to a number of the AQA GCSE History questions to make the demands of the questions clearer for all students. Please refer to the AQA website for more information.

To support you with these changes, this book has been written to match the updated specification.

AUTHOR
Rob Bircher

SERIES EDITOR
Aaron Wilkes

OXFORD
UNIVERSITY PRESS

OXFORD
UNIVERSITY PRESS

Great Clarendon Street, Oxford, OX2 6DP, United Kingdom

Oxford University Press is a department of the University of Oxford. It furthers the University's objective of excellence in research, scholarship, and education by publishing worldwide. Oxford is a registered trade mark of Oxford University Press in the UK and in certain other countries.

© Oxford University Press 2024

The moral rights of the author have been asserted

First published in 2024

All rights reserved. No part of this publication may be reproduced, stored in a retrieval system, transmitted, used for text and data mining, or used for training artificial intelligence, in any form or by any means, without the prior permission in writing of Oxford University Press, or as expressly permitted by law, by licence or under terms agreed with the appropriate reprographics rights organization. Enquiries concerning reproduction outside the scope of the above should be sent to the Rights Department, Oxford University Press, at the address above.

You must not circulate this work in any other form and you must impose this same condition on any acquirer

British Library Cataloguing in Publication Data
Data available

978-1-382-04405-9

10 9 8 7 6 5 4 3 2 1

The manufacturing process conforms to the environmental regulations of the country of origin.

Printed in India by Multivista Global Pvt. Ltd.

Acknowledgements
The publisher and authors would like to thank the following for permission to use photographs and other copyright material:

Photos: p29: National Anthropological Archives, Smithsonian Institution INV 09984800 (Photo Lot 90–1); **p50:** Heritage Images / Getty Images; **p57:** Library of Congress, Geography and Map Division.

Artwork by Moreno Chiacchiera, Kamae Design, Q2A Media, Abel Ippolito, Rudolf Farkas, Martin Sanders, and Oxford University Press.

Every effort has been made to contact copyright holders of material reproduced in this book. Any omissions will be rectified in subsequent printings if notice is given to the publisher.

Contents

Introduction to this Revision Guide 5
Top revision tips 6
Master your exam skills 7
How to master the 'interpretation' questions 8
How to master the 'describe' question 8
How to master the 'in what ways' question 9
How to master the 'bullet points' question 9
AQA GCSE History mark schemes 10
America 1840–1895 Timeline 11

Part one:
Expansion: Opportunities and challenges

1 Indigenous North America 12

    The Plains environment 12
    The 'Great American Desert' 13
    Dealing with a different culture 14
    Manifest Destiny 15

2 Who went west? 16

    The challenges of 'going west' 16
    Migrant farmers 'go west' 17
    Why did Mormons 'go west'? The challenges Mormons faced moving west .. 18
    The California Gold Rush 20
    The Mountain Meadow Massacre 22

3 Indigenous rights and the US government 24

    Early US government policy towards Indigenous nations 24
    Changing relationships with Indigenous nations 25

RECAP | APPLY | REVIEW

Contents

Part two:
Conflict across America

4 Increasing conflict on the Plains — 26

- The Fort Laramie Treaty (1851) 26
- The 'Indian Wars' (1862–1867) 28

5 The American Civil War (1861–1865) — 30

- The background to the Civil War 30
- The impacts of the Civil War 32

Part three:
Consolidation: Forging the nation

6 The aftermath of the Civil War — 34

- The economic impacts of the Civil War 34
- Amendments to the US Constitution 35
- Reconstruction 36

7 Continued settlement of the West — 38

- The Homestead Act (1862) 38
- The Pacific Railroad Act (1862) 40
- Farming the Plains 42

8 Indigenous resistance — 44

- President Grant's Peace Policy 44
- Euro-American attitudes to Indigenous people 46
- The Battle of the Little Big Horn (1876) 48
- Reactions to the Battle of the Little Big Horn 50
- The Dawes Act (1887), Indigenous residential schools 52
- Conditions on reservations, the Wounded Knee Massacre (1890) 54
- Theories about the frontier, Indigenous peoples and the frontier 56

Exam practice: GCSE sample answers 58

- Activity answers guidance 64
- Glossary 71

RECAP   APPLY   REVIEW

Introduction

The **Oxford AQA GCSE History** textbook series has been developed by an expert team led by Jon Cloake and Aaron Wilkes. This matching revision guide offers you step-by-step strategies to master your AQA Period Study: America 1840–1895 exam skills, and the structured revision approach of **Recap, Apply and Review** to prepare you for exam success.

Use the **Progress checklists** on pages 3–4 to keep track of your revision, and use the traffic light feature on each page to monitor your confidence level on each topic. Other exam practice and revision features include **Top revision tips** on page 6, and the **'How to…'** guides for each exam question type on pages 8–9.

RECAP

Each chapter recaps key events and developments through easy-to-digest chunks and visual diagrams. **Key terms** appear in bold and red font; they are defined in the glossary. indicates the relevant Oxford AQA History Student Book pages so you could easily re-read the textbook for further revision.

SUMMARY highlights the most important facts at the end of each chapter.

TIMELINE provides a short list of dates to help you remember key events.

APPLY

Each revision activity is designed to help drill your understanding of facts, and then progress towards applying your knowledge to exam questions.

These targeted revision activities are written specifically for this guide, which will help you apply your knowledge towards the four exam questions in your AQA America 1840–1895 exam paper:

INTERPRETATION ANALYSIS **DESCRIBE** **IN WHAT WAYS** **BULLET POINTS**

 Examiner Tip highlights key parts of an exam question, and gives you hints on how to avoid common mistakes in exams.

 Revision Skills provides different revision techniques. Research shows that using a variety of revision styles can help cement your revision.

 Review gives you helpful reminders about how to check your answers and how to revise further.

REVIEW

Throughout each chapter, you can review and reflect on the work you have done, and find advice on how to further refresh your knowledge.

You can tick off the Review column from the Progress checklists as you work through this revision guide. **Activity answers guidance** and the **Exam practice** sections with full sample student answers also help you to review your own work.

Top revision tips

Getting your revision right

It is perfectly natural to feel anxious when exam time approaches. The best way to keep on top of the stress is to be organised!

3 months to go

Plan: create a realistic revision timetable, and stick to it!
Track your progress: use the Progress checklists (pages 3–4) to help you track your revision. It will help you stick to your revision plan.
Be realistic: revise in regular, small chunks, of around 30 minutes. Reward yourself with 10 minute breaks – you will be amazed how much more you'll remember.
Positive thinking: motivate yourself by turning your negative thoughts to positive ones. Instead of asking *'why can't I remember this topic at all?'* ask yourself *'what different techniques can I try to improve my memory?'*
Organise: make sure you have everything you need – your revision books, coloured pens, index cards, sticky notes, paper, etc. Find a quiet place where you are comfortable. Divide your notes into sections that are easy to use.
Timeline: create a timeline with colour-coded sticky notes, to make sure you remember important dates relating to the three parts of the America 1840–1895 period study (use the Timeline on page 11 as a starting point).
Practise: ask your teachers for practice questions or past papers.

Revision techniques

Using a variety of revision techniques can help you remember information, so try out different methods:

- Make **flashcards**, using both sides of the card to test yourself on key figures, dates and definitions
- **Colour-code** your notebooks
- **Reread** your textbook or copy out your notes
- Create **mind-maps** for complicated topics
- Draw **pictures** and symbols that spring to mind
- Group study
- Find a **buddy** or group to revise with and test you
- Listen to revision **podcasts** or watch revision **clips**
- Work through the **revision activities** in this guide.

Revision tips to help you pass your America 1840–1895 exam

1 month to go

Key groups and concepts: make sure you understand key concepts for this topic, such as Indigenous peoples, expansion, migration, settlement and resistance. If you're unsure, attend revision sessions and ask your teacher.
Identify your weaknesses: which topics or question types are easier and which are more challenging for you? Schedule more time to revise the challenging topics or question types.
Make it stick: find memorable ways to remember chronology, using fun rhymes, or doodles, for example.
Take a break: do something completely different during breaks – listen to music, take a short walk, make a cup of tea, for example.
Check your answers: answer the exam questions in this guide, then check the Activity answers guidance at the end of the guide to practise applying your knowledge to exam questions.
Understand your mark scheme: review the Mark scheme (page 10) for each exam question, and make sure you understand how you will be marked.
Master your exam skills: study and remember the How to master your exam skills steps (pages 7–9) for each AQA question type – it will help you plan your answers quickly!
Time yourself: practise making plans and answering exam questions within the recommended time limits.
Take mock exams seriously: you can learn from them how to manage your time better under exam conditions.
Rest well: make sure your phone and laptop are put away at least an hour before bed. This will help you rest better.

On the big day

Sleep early: don't work through the night; get a good night's sleep.
Be prepared: make sure you know where and when the exam is, and leave plenty of time to get there.
Check: make sure you have all your equipment in advance, including spare pens!
Drink and eat healthily: avoid too much caffeine or junk food. Drinking water is best – if you are 5% dehydrated, then your concentration drops 20%.
Stay focused: don't listen to people who might try to wind you up about what might come up in the exam – they don't know any more than you.
Good luck!

Master your exam skills

Get to grips with your Paper 1: America 1840–1895 Period Study

The Paper 1 exam lasts 2 hours, and you have to answer 10 questions covering two topics. The first six questions (worth 40 marks) will cover America 1840–1895; the last four questions (44 marks) will cover your Conflict and Tension topic. Here, you will find details about what to expect from the first six questions relating to America 1840–1895, and advice on how to master your exam skills.

You should spend about 1 hour in total on the America 1840–1895 questions – see pages 8–9 for how long to spend on each question. **The six questions will always follow this pattern:**

▼ **INTERPRETATION A**

▼ **INTERPRETATION B**

01 How does **Interpretation B** differ from **Interpretation A** about…? Explain your answer based on what it says in **Interpretations A** and **B**. [4 marks]

02 Why might the authors of **Interpretations A** and **B** have a different interpretation about…? Explain your answer using **Interpretations A** and **B** and your contextual knowledge. [4 marks]

03 Which interpretation gives the more convincing opinion about…? Explain your answer based on your contextual knowledge and what it says in **Interpretations A** and **B**. [8 marks]

04 Describe two… [4 marks]

05 In what ways… Explain your answer. [8 marks]

06 Which of the following was the more important reason…
- ☐ _____
- ☐ _____?

Explain your answer with reference to **both** bullet points. [12 marks]

> **REVIEW**
>
> If you find interpretations challenging, look out for the INTERPRETATION ANALYSIS activities throughout this guide to help you revise and drill your understanding of the INTERPRETATION ANALYSIS questions. Look out for the REVISION SKILLS tips too, to inspire you to find the revision strategies that work for you!

REVISION SKILLS

Read the *Conflict and Tension Revision Guide* for help on the last four questions of Paper 1.

EXAMINER TIP

The **caption** for the interpretations is key. It gives you the provenance, which are the details about when or where it was written or said, and the author's background.

EXAMINER TIP

The actual **content** of the interpretations is equally important – you need to read it carefully and consider the reasons why the author might have written/said it, who they were trying to communicate to, and the tone. Don't just think about what it says, think about *how* it is said!

EXAMINER TIP

Question 6 will always have two bullet points referring to factors or events. You need to show you can evaluate by deciding which of the bullet points to argue for. This question is worth 12 marks, so make sure you give yourself enough time to plan and write your essay.

Master your exam skills

How to master the 'interpretation' questions

Here are the steps to consider when answering the three interpretation questions. Remember that each question targets a different aspect of the interpretations.

Question 1

- **Content:** Read the question and the two interpretations carefully, and analyse the contents of both interpretations. What is different in the interpretations? Where does the content differ? Write down at least 2–3 differences. Make sure you refer to both **Interpretations A** and **B**.
- Spend about 5 minutes answering this 4-mark question.

Question 2

- **Context:** This question is about the circumstances in which the interpretations were said/written. What situation was the person in that made them say what they said? Make sure you use the captions (provenances) of each interpretation to help you answer this question.
- Spend about 5 minutes on this 4-mark question.

Question 3

- **Comment:** First, what historical facts can you use to support or challenge each author's view? Use the knowledge you have based on what you've studied about this topic. Again, make sure you comment on both interpretations in turn.
- **Conclude:** Finally, comment on which you find most convincing – which interpretation fits better with what you know about the history of this topic? Your conclusion on which is most convincing should be based on the history that happened, not on who the author is.
- Spend about 10 minutes on this 8-mark question.

How to master the 'describe' question

Here are the steps to consider when answering the 'describe' question.

Question 4

- **Two features:** You have to show what you know and understand about two key features or issues of this period. Make sure you name the two features, then write some historical facts about each of those features.
- Spend about 5 minutes on this 4-mark question.

Master your exam skills

How to master the 'in what ways' question

Here are the steps to consider when answering the 'in what ways' question.

Question 5

- **What changed and what caused the changes:** You have to explain how a particular group of people experienced changes due to developments in this period of America's history. What were the causes of the changes, and what impacts did they have? Name 2–3 changes, causes, or consequences, then write some facts about each change/cause/consequence.
- Spend about 10 minutes on this 8-mark question.

How to master the 'bullet points' question

The last question on America 1840–1895 in Paper 1 will always relate to two bullet points. You have to compare the two things named in the bullet points, and come up with a judgement (conclusion) about which is more important. Here are the steps to consider:

Question 6

- **Read the question carefully:** What topic is the question asking about? The topic is located before the colon. Underline the topic and the dates to help you focus your answer.
- **Plan your essay:** Ask yourself, 'what are the historical facts or concepts I know about how each bullet point affected the topic?' Spend 1–2 minutes drawing a quick mind-map to establish your main arguments/historical evidence on each of the bullet points. Try to structure your essay answer in four paragraphs, starting with an introduction, then two main paragraphs, and a conclusion.
- **Introduce your argument:** Make sure you name the key topic and dates, and the two bullet points.
- **Analyse each bullet:** For each bullet point, write at least one paragraph about why that point may be more important, or what the impact of the bullet point was.
- **Conclude your argument:** It is important to come to a conclusion. Decide (judge) which bullet point you think was more important, and summarise your argument.
- Spend about 20 minutes on this 12-mark question.

> **REVIEW**
>
> You can find sample student answers to each question type in the **Exam Practice** pages at the end of this guide.

> **EXAMINER TIP**
>
> Don't forget you will have to answer four more questions relating to your Conflict and Tension topic in Paper 1. Ensure you leave enough time to complete both sections of Paper 1! You are advised to spend about 1 hour on your Conflict and Tension topic in the exam.

AQA GCSE History mark schemes

Below are simplified versions of the AQA mark schemes, to help you understand the marking criteria for your **Paper 1: America 1840–1895** exam.

Level	Interpretation question 1
2	• Developed analysis of the content of the two interpretations. • Differences are explained with relevant facts. [3–4 marks]
1	• Simple analysis of the content of one or two interpretations. • Differences are named. [1–2 marks]

Level	Interpretation question 2
2	• Developed analysis of the provenance of the two interpretations. • Differences in the provenance (e.g. time of writing, place, circumstances, audience) are explained with relevant facts/understanding. [3–4 marks]
1	• Simple analysis of the provenance of the interpretation(s). • Differences in the provenance (e.g. time of writing, place, circumstances, audience) are named. [1–2 marks]

Level	Interpretation question 3
4	• Complex evaluation of the two interpretations. • Argument about which interpretation is more/less convincing is shown throughout the answer, supported by relevant facts/understanding. [7–8 marks]
3	• Developed evaluation of the two interpretations. • Argument is stated about which interpretation is more/less convincing. Answer is supported by relevant facts/understanding. [5–6 marks]
2	• Simple answer of one interpretation (there may be a basic analysis of the other interpretation). • Answer is supported with relevant facts/understanding. [3–4 marks]
1	• Basic answer on one or two interpretations. • Some facts/understanding are shown. [1–2 marks]

Level	Describe question
2	• Answer explains relevant facts and understanding. [3–4 marks]
1	• Answer names some relevant facts. [1–2 marks]

Level	In what ways question
4	• Complex explanation of two or more changes. • A range of accurate, detailed and relevant facts are shown. [7–8 marks]
3	• Developed explanation of two or more changes/consequences. • A range of accurate, relevant facts are shown. [5–6 marks]
2	• Simple explanation of one change. • Specific relevant facts are shown. [3–4 marks]
1	• Basic explanation of change(s). • Some basic related facts are shown. [1–2 marks]

Level	Bullet points question
4	• Complex explanation of two bullet points. • A range of accurate and detailed facts that are relevant to the question. [10–12 marks]
3	• Developed explanation of two bullet points. • A range of accurate facts shown that are relevant to the question. [7–9 marks]
2	• Simple explanation of one or two bullet points. • Specific facts shown that are relevant to the question. [4–6 marks]
1	• Basic explanation of one or two bullet points. • Some basic facts shown that are relevant to the question. [1–3 marks]

America 1840–1895 Timeline

The symbols represent different types of event as follows:

economic   political   conflict and resistance   social and cultural

1830 ✕ The 'Trail of Tears' begins: a 20-year period when more than 125,000 Indigenous people are forced to leave their homelands and journey west.

1834 📜 The US government passes the Indian Trade and Intercourse Act, establishing the Permanent Indian Frontier

1847 👫 July – Mormon settlers arrive in the Great Salt Lake Valley

1849 💰 The California Gold Rush

1851 📜 September – the first Fort Laramie Treaty is agreed

1857 ✕ September – The Mountain Meadow Massacre occurs

1861 ✕ April – The Civil War begins

1862 📜 May – US government passes the Homestead Act

1864 ✕ November – Sand Creek Massacre occurs

1865 ✕ April – The Civil War ends

1865 📜 December – The Thirteenth Amendment is ratified, abolishing slavery in the USA

1866 📜 April – The US government passes the Civil Rights Act, making everyone born in the USA a US citizen and giving all citizens the same legal rights

1866 ✕ July – Red Cloud's War begins

1866 ✕ December – Fetterman's Trap

1868 📜 April – The second Fort Laramie Treaty is agreed

1874 💰 July–August – Gold discovered in the Black Hills, the sacred lands of Paha Sapa

1876 ✕ June – The Battle of the Little Big Horn takes place. The Lakota name for the battle is the 'Battle of the Greasy Grass'

1887 📜 February – The US government passes the Dawes Act, which aims to assimilate Indigenous peoples

1890 👫 The Ghost Dance movement spreads across the Plains

1890 👫 June – The US Census reports that there is no longer an American frontier

1890 ✕ December – The Wounded Knee Massacre occurs

1944 👫 The National Congress of American Indians (NCAI) is formed, bringing together 50 Indigenous nations to protect Indigenous rights and to improve the lives of Indigenous people in the USA

America 1840–1895 Expansion and Consolidation

CHAPTER 1

Indigenous North America

RECAP

The Plains environment

Indigenous people were living in North America for thousands of years before the first Europeans arrived. The Plains were a challenging environment for humans to live in, but Indigenous people had developed sophisticated ways to unlock the resources of the Plains.

The Plains: a challenging place to live

- The climate was dry. There wasn't enough rain to grow enough food to live on, and rivers were scarce so crops couldn't be irrigated. There was water, but it was deep underground.
- The dry climate meant trees were rare, so there was very little wood for building, tools or fuel.
- Summers were hot, and violent storms were frequent. Winters were very cold, especially in the northern Plains.
- The Plains were covered by grass. Huge herds of animals grazed the grass, but they were fast-moving and travelled vast distances, making them hard to hunt on foot.

> This book uses the terms 'Indigenous peoples' and 'Indigenous nations' to refer to the original inhabitants of the Americas, sometimes known as Native Americans. Sources and interpretations from the period 1840–1895 typically refer to 'Indians' for these people and nations.

Unlocking the resources of the Plains: bison

Horse nations, such as the Lakota, could live on the Plains because they developed skills to hunt **bison** on horseback. They used every part of the bison, which was their main source of food, clothing and shelter.

- Bison **hide** was used to make leather, which was then made into clothes, saddles, bags and **tipis**.
- Dried bison dung was used as fuel for fires.
- Bison bladders were used for storing water or food.
- Bison bones were used to make arrowheads, needles and dice.
- Dried bison meat, bison fat and berries were used to make pemmican, a food that could be stored and eaten in winter.
- Thick furry bison hide was made into warm robes, which could be traded with other Indigenous **nations** and with **Euro-Americans**.
- Bison fat was used to make soap and to cook with.

Unlocking the resources of the Plains: tipis

Nomadic horse nations, such as the Lakota, moved across the Plains to find the scattered resources they needed. Tipis provided the ideal housing.

- Tipis were quick to set up and to dismantle. They were also light, making them easy to transport.
- Tipis were made of waterproof hides and had flaps for ventilation.
- Fires were lit inside tipis so they were warm in winter. A hole at the top let out smoke.
- Tipis were in the shape of a cone, which made them sturdy and able to cope with storms and strong winds.

Unlocking the resources of the Plains: social organisation and roles

Nomadic horse nations, like the Lakota, were organised to meet the challenges of living on the Plains.

- Bands: For most of the year, resources were too scarce for whole nations to live in one place. Instead, nations split into **bands** of around 100 people, which travelled to find the resources they needed.
- Chiefs: Each band had a chief, chosen for their specific skills, such as knowledge of Plains resources. Chiefs sorted out disputes, so that everyone could work together.
- Councils: Chiefs came together in **councils** to make decisions for the whole nation. The Lakota Nation was also part of the **Oceti Sakowin**, and the leaders from the seven nations of the Oceti Sakowin met to discuss issues and resolve crises, such as war.
- **Warrior societies**: These military units defended the band and its territory from raids and raided other nations. Warrior societies also organised big events such as bison hunts.
- Individual roles: Men and women had some specific roles to ensure the skilled work was completed that enabled the band to survive over the winter. For example, men hunted and protected the community, and women prepared food and products for trade. Men and women also shared many roles too, such as childcare, and took on each other's roles when needed.

The 'Great American Desert'

Euro-Americans (people of European heritage who settled in North America) saw the Plains as a desert where it was impossible to live. They called the Plains the 'Great American Desert'.

- Euro-Americans couldn't survive on the Plains without farming, but it was too dry for farming until underground water became accessible in the mid-nineteenth century.
- Euro-Americans preferred to settle in families, but a family wasn't a large enough group to do all the jobs needed to survive.
- There was no wood for building, tools or fuel, and Euro-Americans hadn't got the skills to survive without timber.
- Euro-Americans wanted to settle in one place that belonged just to them, but you needed to move from place to place to find the resources you needed to survive on the Plains.

APPLY

DESCRIBE

a Aspects of the Plains environment are listed below. Complete the table by describing why each aspect made living on the Plains challenging, and how Indigenous nations dealt with the challenges.

The Plains environment	Why a challenge?	How Indigenous nations dealt with it
Dry climate		
Few trees		
Cold winters		
Fast-moving animals		
Scattered resources		

b Why do you think Euro-Americans call the Plains the 'Great American Desert' when Indigenous people were so successful at living there? Write your viewpoint in no more than 50 words.

c **EXAM QUESTION** Describe two problems faced by Indigenous nations living on the Plains.

REVISION SKILLS

Reading through information and highlighting it won't do much to help you remember it. You need to apply what you've read and then it will stick!

EXAMINER TIP

Make sure the problems you talk about are relevant to the people and/or situation that the question asks about.

RECAP

Dealing with a different culture

There were important differences between Indigenous cultures and the settler cultures of Euro-Americans.

Land

- Indigenous nations such as the Lakota believed that everything, including land, was created by the Great Spirit, *Wakan Tanka*, for people to use. People should protect and care for the land entrusted to their nation, but land couldn't belong to anyone.
- Euro-Americans believed one person could buy and own land, change it however they wanted, and decide that no one else was allowed to use it. They believed land should be exploited to make as much money as possible.

▼ **A** *Euro-Americans took Indigenous land and divided it into separate plots owned by individuals*

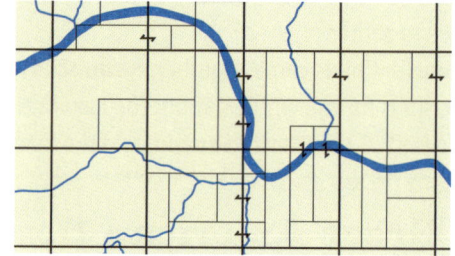

Beliefs

- Different Indigenous nations have different beliefs. For example, the Lakota believe that *Wakan Tanka* rules over everything and that there are spirits in everything, including animals. Crises such as disease and famine come when people do not respect the Earth and its spirits.
- European settlers, most of whom were Christians, had little respect for Indigenous beliefs. Some Christian settlers believed they needed to convert Indigenous people to their own religion.

Cultural differences

Nations and leaders

- Indigenous nations are **sovereign nations**, and Euro-Americans recognised this when they negotiated treaties with Indigenous nations to take their land.
- However, Euro-Americans did not understand the relationship between chiefs and their nations. They thought that if the leader of a nation signed a law, then the law would be obeyed by all the people of that nation. However, in many Indigenous nations, decisions needed to be agreed by everyone and be in the interests of everyone. If a band thought a chief's decision was wrong, they ignored it.

Conflict

- Conflict was common between Indigenous nations on the Plains because resources were scarce: the main aim of conflict was to gain control of scarce resources.
- Raids were how young people won respect and prestige, but conflicts were carefully controlled because everyone had a role in helping the band survive. **Counting coup** was a way of disgracing an enemy without killing them: the aim was to strike them with a coup stick like the one in the picture and then get away without being hurt yourself.
- Euro-Americans had a very different view of conflict. European-style warfare aimed to fight until enough of the enemy had been killed for a victory to be declared.

Identity

- Indigenous nations are proud of their identities and many have a tradition of 'adopting' individuals from outside their culture into their nations.
- Euro-Americans wanted to 'civilise' Indigenous people, stopping them from living their traditional ways of life and forcing them to take on European customs and cultures.

Manifest Destiny

The United States of America (USA) came into being in 1776 when 13 colonies in the East declared independence from Britain. The USA then expanded by taking land from Indigenous nations.

In the 1840s, as the USA grew, some US politicians and journalists said it was the USA's **Manifest Destiny** to expand; that God had given the USA a mission to expand its territory, culture and values to all of America, including even to take over all of Canada and Mexico.

Although the USA did not take over all of Canada and Mexico, the idea of Manifest Destiny was influential:

- Settlers claimed the right to take land from Indigenous people because they would do something 'useful' with it.
- Even when the law of the USA protected Indigenous rights, the government still took land away from Indigenous people, because the USA 'must' be allowed to expand.
- Many in the USA believed that it was the 'destiny' of Indigenous people to become 'civilised' or to disappear.

SUMMARY

- The Plains were a challenging environment for humans to live in, but Indigenous people had developed sophisticated ways to access the resources of the Plains.
- Euro-Americans called the Plains the 'Great American Desert'. Unlike Indigenous people's ways of life, Euro-American ways of living were not adapted to the Plains environment.
- There were important differences between Indigenous cultures and the settler cultures of Euro-Americans.
- In the 1840s, as the USA grew, some US politicians and journalists said it was the USA's Manifest Destiny to expand by taking land from Indigenous nations.

APPLY

INTERPRETATION ANALYSIS

Read this interpretation.

▼ **INTERPRETATION A** *Adapted from an article called 'Recollections and Opinions of an Old Pioneer', published in 1904 in the magazine of the Oregon History Society. A 'pioneer' is a term for a settler who is one of the first non-Indigenous people to reach an area, and this interpretation is about the expansion of the USA in Oregon in the Far West:*

> I saw that a great American community would grow up, in the space of a few years, upon the shores of the distant Pacific. At that time Oregon Territory was claimed by both Great Britain and the United States. The only way to settle the matter was to fill the country with American citizens. If we could only show, by a practical test, that American emigrants could safely make their way across the continent to Oregon with their wagons, teams, cattle and families, then there would be no doubt as to who owned the country.

a The author talks about the need to 'settle the matter' of Oregon. What problem needed to be sorted out? (Hint: who is claiming Oregon at this time?)
b How does the author think the problem should be sorted?
c Why might the author, 'an old pioneer', have this view of migration?
d Describe how his view could be linked to Manifest Destiny.

REVISION SKILLS

An interpretation is a person's view about an event that happened in the past. It might differ from another person's view about the same event, and your job in the exam includes identifying differences between two people's views and explaining them based on what you already know.

CHAPTER 2 Who went west?

RECAP

The challenges of 'going west'

In the 1840s, the USA expanded massively. A treaty with Britain in 1846 meant Oregon Territory became part of the USA. Then, in 1848, Mexico gave up California, Utah and parts of New Mexico to the USA after losing a war.

The US government wanted US citizens to move to the new territories in the Far West of America, but the journey by sea was long and expensive. Getting there by land would be quicker and cheaper, but migrants needed a reliable route through the Rocky Mountains.

The Oregon Trail

In 1825, a mountain man called Jedediah Smith told people about the South Pass, a path through the Rocky Mountains. It became part of the Oregon Trail, a reliable 2,000 miles overland trail from Independence in Missouri to Oregon Territory.

The Oregon Trail was one of three main trails used to travel west. These trails, like most of the routes used by Euro-American migrants, were often based on Indigenous routes and were only 'discovered' by mountain men because they had been shown them by Indigenous people.

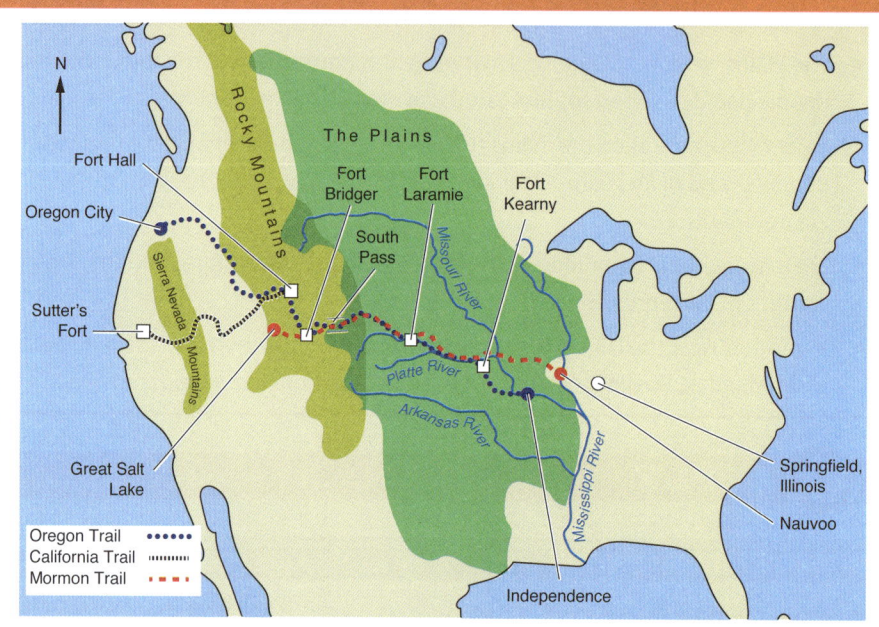

The journey

Migrants used wagons to carry everything they needed to set up a new farm in the Far West. The wagons could weigh 2 tonnes. They often broke, and migrants needed to push them up hills.

Accidents were common. Migrants were sometimes crushed under wagon wheels.

Oxen were often used to pull the heavy wagons. They were strong and didn't get injured as easily as horses, but they were very slow. Wagons might only travel 3 miles in a day.

Time was the biggest challenge. Migrants had to make it through the mountains before snow blocked their way.

Livestock needed grass to eat. That meant migrants couldn't travel until spring when there was enough grass.

Diseases spread quickly through wagon trains. Cholera spread when migrants drank water from places where other migrants had gone to the toilet.

Migrant farmers 'go west'

By 1869, more than 400,000 people had migrated to the Far West along the Oregon Trail, many of them farmers. Why did they make this long journey?

Pull factors to the Far West

 In the 1840s, Euro-American migrants could claim a square mile of land in the Far West for free.

 California and Oregon had a good climate for farming, and fertile soil.

 People who had made the journey west encouraged others to join them.

 In 1848, gold was discovered in California and people rushed there to get rich.

Push factors from the East

 There was an economic depression in the East in the 1840s and people found it hard to make a living, especially farmers in states like Ohio.

 Land was expensive in the East, making it hard to grow enough crops to make money.

 Many of the families that migrated to Oregon had moved several times before to try to find better, cheaper farmland. Migrating wasn't new to them.

APPLY

DESCRIBE

a Copy this table and then complete it from memory.

Reasons why migrant farmers migrated west in the 1840s	Brief description of the reason	Was it a pull factor or a push factor?
'Free land' in the Far West		
Farming conditions in the Far West		
Stories from migrants who had made the trip west		
Discovery of gold in the Far West		
Economic depression in the East		
Expensive land in the East		

b Suggest reasons why the Oregon Trail made it possible for more people to migrate west.

c  Describe two problems faced by people in the East of the USA that encouraged migration west.

EXAMINER TIP

Both of your problems need to be problems experienced by people living in the East.

RECAP

Why did Mormons 'go west'?

The **Mormons** are a religious group that identify as Christians. In 1846, Brigham Young decided to lead a group of Mormons to the Great Salt Lake Valley in Utah, which at the time was not US territory. This was because the Mormons faced discrimination and religious persecution in the USA.

- Mormons had tried to set up communities in the USA where they could live according to their beliefs.
- But many non-Mormons resented the way lots of Mormons moved to their communities and often took control of local government. They also said Mormon beliefs were blasphemous, and criticised the way some Mormon men had more than one wife (marrying more than one person at a time is called polygamy).
- The US government also did not like the way Mormons wanted to govern themselves. For example, the Mormon community of Nauvoo had its own **militia**, the Nauvoo Legion.
- Mormons were often attacked by mobs. In 1844, Mormon leader Joseph Smith was murdered by a mob.

By autumn 1846, 5,000 Mormons were camped on Indigenous land by the Missouri River. They stayed there for the winter, ready to continue their journey in the spring.

In April 1847, Young set out on the 1,000-mile trip with a small group of 150 called the Pioneer Band. They left signs for the rest of the Mormons to follow, reaching the Great Salt Lake Valley in July 1847.

The challenges Mormons faced moving west

Young knew the challenges of the journey west and planned the migration carefully.

A reliable route

Young used experienced trail guides to find the safest and quickest route to the Great Salt Lake Valley. To avoid mixing with non-Mormons, the new route went along the north bank of the Platte River rather than the south bank like the Oregon Trail.

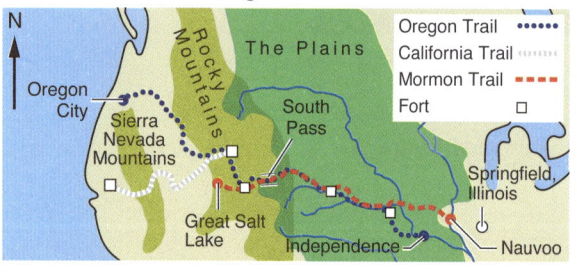

Military-style organisation

Discipline was strict so everything necessary got done and the migrants were not delayed. For example:

- Captains led groups of 100 wagons and lieutenants led groups of ten wagons.
- Migrants woke early, at 5:00am when the bugle sounded, and the wagon trains were ready to leave by 7:00am. There were regular rest stops throughout the day so people and animals did not get too tired.
- At night, wagons were corralled, with livestock kept safe in the middle.

Thinking ahead

Families gathered sticks for firewood as they walked. They planted potatoes along the way so migrants following them would have food to eat.

Settling in the Great Salt Lake Valley

The Mormons faced many challenges adapting their way of life to Utah's environment.

Problems	Solutions
The Great Salt Lake was too salty to use to irrigate crops or as drinking water.	Mormons copied Indigenous techniques, such as making dams in creeks to store fresh water.
There were very few trees, so very little timber to use for buildings.	Mormons copied Indigenous building techniques, using adobe (mud and straw) to build houses.
Young wanted the settlements of the Great Salt Lake Valley to be self-sufficient so Mormons did not have to interact with people from the USA.	Each family was given half an acre of land to build a home and plant food. A square mile of fields for crops surrounded each settlement.
Thousands of workers were needed to build Salt Lake City, but Mormons back in the East were poor and couldn't afford the trip.	The Perpetual Emigration Fund was set up in 1849 to raise money to help Mormons migrate to the Great Salt Lake Valley.

INTERPRETATION ANALYSIS

Read this interpretation.

▼ **INTERPRETATION A** *Adapted from a speech by Brigham Young, made in 1870. By 1870, over 70,000 Mormons had migrated to the Great Salt Lake Valley, and built around 90 settlements in Utah Territory. The first transcontinental railroad was completed in 1869, ending the need for migrants to travel by wagon:*

> Since the day that we first trod the soil of these valleys, have we received any assistance from our neighbors? No, we have not. We have built our homes, our cities, have made our farms, have dug our canals and water ditches, have subdued this barren country, have fed the stranger, have clothed the naked, have immigrated the poor from foreign lands, have placed them in a condition to make all comfortable and have made some rich. We have fed the Indians to the amount of thousands of dollars yearly, have clothed them in part, and have sustained several Indian wars, and now we have built thirty-seven miles of railroad.

a   'subdued this barren country' means making the land around the Great Salt Lake into farmland. In your view, how convincing is this part of Young's speech? Use evidence to back up your answer.

b   'immigrated the poor from foreign lands' means bringing people from Europe to help colonise the Great Salt Lake area. How convincing is this part of Young's speech? Can you back up your answer with evidence?

c   'placed them in a condition to make all comfortable' refers to the way the Mormons settled the Great Salt Lake Valley. In your view, how convincing is this part of the speech? What evidence could you use to back up your view?

d   Brigham Young talks about supporting Indigenous people. How convincing do you find that claim? What have you learned about the interactions between Mormons and Indigenous people that challenges Young's view?

BULLET POINTS

a   Read pages 16 and 17 and write down all the economic reasons people migrated west in the 1840s.

b   **Which of the following was the more important reason why migration west increased in the USA after 1840:**
- **economic reasons**
- **religious reasons?**

Explain your answer with reference to both bullet points.

EXAMINER TIP

'How convincing' means 'how well does this interpretation agree with what I already know about this topic'. If an interpretation does not agree with what you already know, then it will be less convincing than one that does.

EXAMINER TIP

The bullet points in this question probably make you think of Mormons for religious reasons and gold rush migrants and farmers facing economic depression for economic reasons. One way to decide which was more important could be simply to compare the numbers who migrated west in the 1840s for religious and for economic reasons.

America 1840–1895 Expansion and Consolidation   19

RECAP

The California Gold Rush

In January 1848, at Sutter's Mill in California, James Marshall spotted rock glinting in a trench being dug by Indigenous bonded workers (Indigenous people who were bound to work for the mill owner by agreement).

News of the discovery spread and there was a gold rush:

- In 1849, around 90,000 people arrived in California to prospect for gold, about half arriving by sea and half by land using the California Trail.
- By 1855, the population of California had increased to 300,000.

Two-thirds of migrants were from the USA, the rest were from countries all round the world; for example, 20,000 Chinese men arrived in San Francisco in 1852.

Most of the migrants were men: of the 40,000 migrants arriving by sea in 1849, only around 700 were women.

The California Gold Rush had significant consequences.

Consequences for US expansion

- The rapid increase in population meant California became a US state in 1850.
- Most migrants did not find gold, but California's economy grew. There were huge profits for shipping companies, businesses supplying migrants boomed, and failed prospectors started farming or worked as farm labourers.
- California's rapid economic growth strengthened Euro-Americans' belief in Manifest Destiny.

▼ **A** *A map showing the US states in 1850*

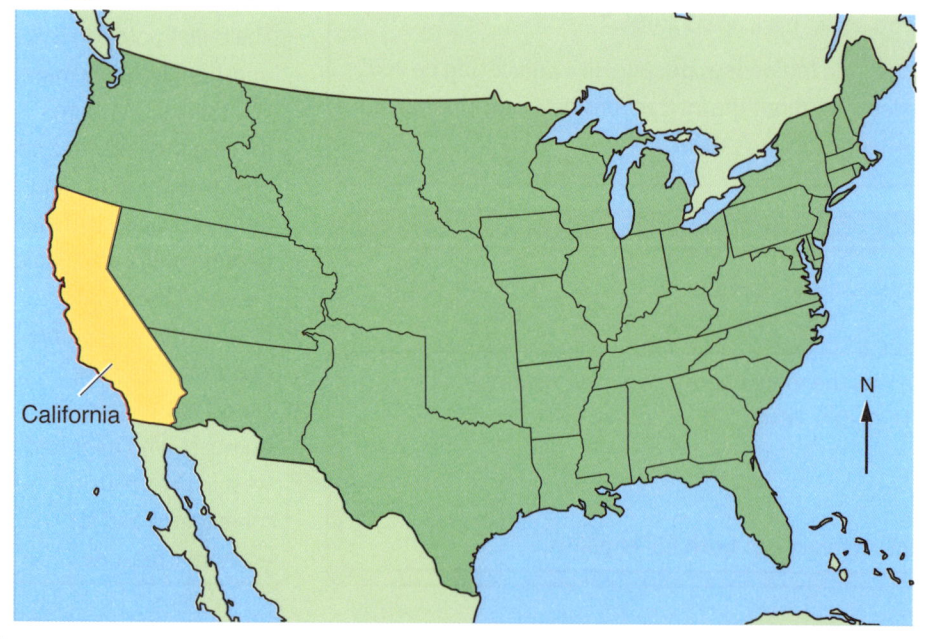

Consequences for Chinese migrants

- Euro-American miners were strongly opposed to Chinese miners and used violence to force them away from new claims.
- However, Chinese miners worked extremely hard, and succeeded in getting gold out of sites other miners had abandoned.
- There were hundreds of violent attacks on Chinese migrants, and law officers did nothing to protect them. As a result, many Chinese people went to work building the new railroads.

Consequences for Indigenous people

Indigenous people suffered greatly as a result of violence by miners, diseases spread by the new arrivals and thefts of their land. The Indigenous population of California was 100,000 before the Gold Rush; by 1870 it was 30,000.

In order to mine for gold, Euro-Americans stole land by defrauding, tricking or forcing Indigenous nations off their land.

- Euro-Americans shot Indigenous people who they said were a threat to settlers. 20,000 Indigenous people were killed between 1848 and 1870.
- Settlers were allowed, by law, to capture Indigenous people to use as bonded workers and to 'adopt' Indigenous children, using them as workers too.
- The environmental consequences of mining destroyed the habitats that Indigenous people relied on: mining camps drove away animals, land was deforested, streams and rivers were silted up or poisoned with chemicals.

APPLY

IN WHAT WAYS

a Copy this table and then complete it from memory.

	Impacts of the California Gold Rush
Indigenous people	
Chinese miners	
Euro-Americans	

b **EXAM QUESTION** In what ways were the lives of people living in the USA affected by the California Gold Rush?

EXAMINER TIP

Compare the impacts of the California Gold Rush for different groups of people. Examples of groups you could consider when answering 'in what ways' questions include: old and young, women and men, Indigenous people and Euro-Americans, Black Americans and white Americans. In this case, it would be useful to compare the experiences of Indigenous people, Chinese miners and Euro-Americans.

RECAP

The Mountain Meadow Massacre

The Mountain Meadow Massacre happened in 1857, at a time of conflict between the US government and Mormons living in Utah Territory.

The events of the Mountain Meadow Massacre

In 1850, the US government made Utah into a US territory. Although the US government appointed Brigham Young as the first governor of the territory, tensions increased between the government and the Mormons.

The Mormons wanted to live independently and follow their own laws and practices, but the US government would not allow this. In 1857, the US government decided to replace Brigham Young with a non-Mormon governor.

In July 1857, US President James Buchanan ordered 25,000 soldiers to go to Utah Territory to make sure US laws were being obeyed.

In August 1857, Brigham Young declared **martial law**. The Mormons also encouraged local Indigenous people to raid migrant wagon trains.

Also in August, the Fancher party of migrants arrived in the Great Salt Lake Valley. The Mormons refused to sell the Fancher party any food or let them graze their livestock. Both sides became extremely angry.

The Fancher party camped at Mountain Meadow. A Mormon called John D. Lee and the Nauvoo Legion attacked them, disguised as Indigenous people.

The attacks went on for several weeks. Then, on 11 September 1857, some Mormons tricked the Fancher party into abandoning their defensive position. One-hundred and twenty people were massacred, including children.

The Mormons covered up the massacre, then tried to blame it on local Indigenous people. However, other migrants passing through saw the bodies and heard rumours. They reported the crime to newspapers in California.

Twenty years later, John D. Lee was convicted for leading the massacre and was executed at Mountain Meadow.

The aftermath of the Mountain Meadow Massacre

The Mountain Meadow Massacre was part of a series of conflicts often referred to as the Utah War. By 1858, around 30,000 Mormons were preparing to burn their settlements in Utah and migrate south in protest.

The US government wanted to avoid a crisis. President Buchanan said the US government would pardon any Mormon who had taken part in the conflict; he also promised not to interfere in Mormon religious affairs, and said he would take the army out of Utah, as long as the Mormon leadership stopped rebelling against the US government. Brigham Young agreed and the tensions came to an end.

SB | 18–29 | Revision progress

SUMMARY

- The USA expanded massively in the 1840s and the US government wanted US citizens to move to the new territories in the Far West.
- By 1869, more than 400,000 people had migrated to the Far West along the Oregon Trail, many of them farmers. Migrants still faced many challenges on their journey.
- Facing discrimination and religious persecution in the USA, Mormons migrated to the Great Salt Lake Valley in 1847.
- The California Gold Rush occurred in 1849 and, by 1855, the population of California had increased to 300,000 people. This had positive consequences for US expansion and for some migrants, but devastating consequences for Indigenous people.
- Tensions increased between Mormons and the US government after the Great Salt Lake Valley became part of the USA in 1850. These tensions led to the Mountain Meadow Massacre in 1857.

 APPLY

BULLET POINTS

a Copy and complete the timeline below, adding details about the points of conflict between Mormons and other Euro-Americans. The first two dates have been done for you.

1830 — The *Book of Mormon* is published. Many non-Mormons say it is blasphemous.

1831 — Mormons move to Kirtland. Many people, most of whom have very little money, join them. Existing Kirtland residents are unhappy and are worried about being outnumbered.

1841 — The Nauvoo Legion is formed. The US government is unhappy because…

1856 — US politicians criticise polygamy among Mormons. Polygamy is…

1857 — President Buchanan sends soldiers to Utah Territory. The soldiers are sent because…

1857 — The Mountain Meadow Massacre takes place. It occurs because…

b Which of the following was the more important reason why there was conflict between Mormons and the US government:
- differences in ways of life
- the actions of the US government?

Explain your answer with reference to **both** bullet points.

REVIEW

This timeline involves some events from earlier in this book: look back at pages 18 and 19.

EXAMINER TIP

A period study, like America 1840–1895, is a detailed study of a country over a period of around 50 years. Make sure you can make connections between different topics across the period so you can answer questions like this, which covers different aspects of the Mormon migration.

America 1840–1895 Expansion and Consolidation   23

CHAPTER 3 Indigenous rights and the US government

RECAP

Early US government policy towards Indigenous nations

Early nineteenth century

US government policy encouraged Indigenous people to live like 'civilised' Euro-Americans. Some nations, such as the Cherokee, decided to accept some Euro-American customs to avoid conflict.

The Indian Removal Act (1830)

The Indian Removal Act of 1830 permitted the US government to make treaties with Indigenous nations to swap Indigenous land in the East for land in 'Indian Territory'.

More than 125,000 Indigenous people were forced to leave their homes between 1830 and 1850. Thousands died on the 'Trail of Tears' to 'Indian Territory', including 4,000 Cherokee. Euro-Americans rushed in to grab the land Indigenous people were made to leave.

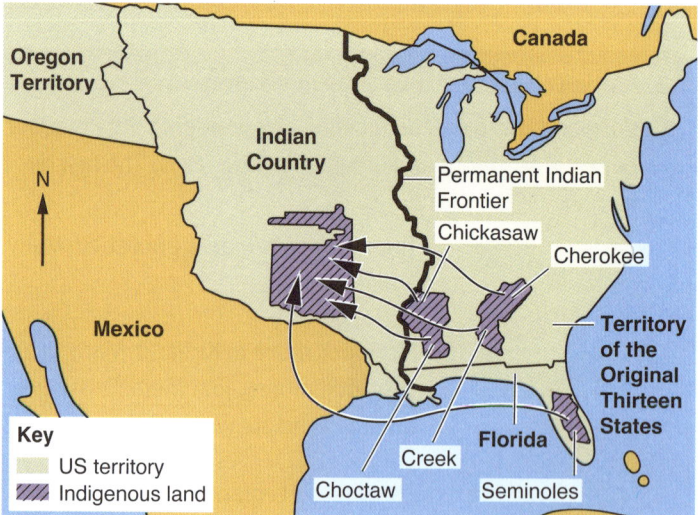

▼ **A** *A map showing 'Indian Country' and the Permanent Indian Frontier, and where Indigenous nations forced to leave their homes in the East travelled to*

The Permanent Indian Frontier (1834)

The Indian Trade and Intercourse Act of 1834 divided the **unorganised territory** of the Plains ('Indian Country') from the US states in the East.

A line of forts was built along the Permanent Indian Frontier to keep Indigenous and non-Indigenous people separate.

Crossing the Permanent Indian Frontier

By the time of the California Gold Rush in 1849, hundreds of thousands of Euro-American migrants were crossing the Permanent Indian Frontier to reach the Far West.

Some Indigenous bands raided migrant wagon trains. The trespassing migrants had horses, cattle, guns and ammunition, which were all very valuable to horse nations.

In response, migrants demanded that the US Army protect them as they travelled through 'Indian Country'.

The Indian Appropriations Act (1851)

The US government changed its policy. It began making treaties with Indigenous nations, in which Indigenous nations agreed to stay away from migrant trails in return for money.

In 1851, the Indian Appropriations Act provided money to set up **reservations**. Indigenous nations were persuaded to give up all but a small part of their territory in return for money and supplies, as well as protection from the US government.

Changing relationships with Indigenous nations

Indigenous people were made to be dependent on the US government by reservation policies.

- **Indian agents**, who were US government officials, supervised reservations and controlled the supplies that reached Indigenous people. They had the power, not chiefs chosen by the people.
- Reservation treaties paid Indigenous nations an annuity (a fixed amount of money paid every year) or goods – such as clothing – of the same value, in return for giving up large areas of their land and moving to reservations. But the Indian agents could decide not to pay annuities, or hold them back, if they decided that reservation rules had been broken.
- The US government wanted Indigenous nations to learn to grow their own food. However, land chosen for reservations was often very difficult to farm. Nations on reservations frequently depended on government food rations to survive.
- Some nations, such as the Lakota, remained independent and free in the 1850s. They did not rely on the US government for anything.

SUMMARY

- In 1834, the Permanent Indian Frontier divided the unorganised territory of the Plains ('Indian Country') from the US states in the East.
- Most of those migrating to the Far West in the 1840s travelled across the Permanent Indian Frontier.
- In 1851, the US government changed its policy towards Indigenous nations and began establishing reservations.

APPLY

IN WHAT WAYS

a What were Indian agents and annuities and how did they affect the lives of some Indigenous people?

b Copy and complete the table below to compare the lives of Indigenous people living on reservations with the traditional ways of life of the Lakota in 1851.

	Indigenous people living on reservations	Members of the Lakota Nation living independently on the Plains
Food	Encouraged to learn how to farm like Europeans, but frequently depended on government food rations.	
Leadership		A band was led by a chief chosen by the people. Leaders from the seven nations of the Oceti Sakowin met to discuss issues and resolve crises.

c **EXAM QUESTION** In what ways were the lives of Indigenous people affected by the US government's reservation policy from 1851?

REVIEW

Think back to your revision of Indigenous North America (pages 12–14) as you complete the table for the Lakota Nation.

EXAMINER TIP

Try to discuss at least two different ways the lives of Indigenous people were affected by the reservation policy, and provide detailed information about both ways.

 **CHAPTER 4** Increasing conflict on the Plains

 **RECAP**

The Fort Laramie Treaty (1851)

The Fort Laramie Treaty of 1851 was signed by the US government and eight Indigenous nations, including the Lakota.

- The Indigenous nations wanted compensation for the migrants who had been crossing their lands for years, especially since the number of migrants travelling across the Plains had increased significantly because of the California Gold Rush.
- The US government abandoned the policy of a Permanent Indian Frontier. Instead, it moved to a policy of concentration: concentrating Indigenous nations within the borders of their own separate territories, away from the overland trails. It also hoped to avoid war with the powerful horse nations of the Plains and wanted to reduce conflict between the eight nations.

The Indigenous nations agreed to:
End the fighting between the eight nations
Allow migrants to travel through their lands in safety
Allow the government to build roads through their territory and construct military forts
Pay compensation if any individuals or bands from their nation attacked migrants passing through their territory
Accept the boundaries of their territories as set out by the treaty

The US government agreed to:
Protect the eight nations from 'depredations' by US citizens; from attacks, raids or attempts to steal from the nations
Pay the nations an annuity of $50,000 for 50 years (this was later reduced to ten years), in money for the first five years and then in goods such as food and other goods to sell, livestock and farming equipment
Delay payment of the annuity if nations broke the terms of the treaty

How successful was the Fort Laramie Treaty (1851)?

The Fort Laramie Treaty of 1851 was not successful.

Indigenous nations

Indigenous nations did not get what they wanted. They kept to the terms of the treaty, but migrant settlers had very little respect for their rights and the US government rarely acted to prevent migrant settlers breaking the terms of the treaty.

The US government

The US government wanted to avoid conflict but, by 1862, many Indigenous bands decided they had no other choice but to fight back. The conflicts that followed were, at the time, called the 'Indian Wars'. The US government's policy of concentration had failed.

S B 38–43 Revision progress

APPLY

INTERPRETATION ANALYSIS

Read this interpretation.

▼ **INTERPRETATION A** *Adapted from an extract from a speech made in 1870 by Secretary of the Interior, Jacob Dolson Cox, to a delegation of Indigenous people led by Red Cloud of the Lakota Nation, who had come to report non-payment of annuities and other challenges on reservations. Here Cox talks about the Fort Laramie Treaty of 1851, in which General Sherman led the negotiations for the USA. The Lakota Nation was often referred to as the Sioux at this time.*

> When our people grew so fast as to crowd upon the plains, we wanted to find a place for the Sioux to live, where they would not be disturbed, and for that reason our great soldier, General Sherman, made the treaty to give them the country which they now have, and to take our own people out of it, so they might live there alone. Lately, some of our young people wanted to go there again to look for the gold in the hills, but the President refused to let them go, saying that it had been promised to the Sioux, and they must keep it.

a How accurately does the interpretation describe the US government's aims for the Fort Laramie Treaty of 1851, and the terms agreed? What, if anything, is incorrect or has been left out?

b How accurately does the interpretation describe how successfully the Fort Laramie Treaty of 1851 fulfilled the US government's aims?

BULLET POINTS

a Here are two true statements about the Fort Laramie Treaty of 1851. Can the same things be said about the Permanent Indian Frontier? Did US government policy change? Explain your thinking.
- The Fort Laramie Treaty of 1851 aimed to keep Indigenous people and non-Indigenous people away from each other.
- The Fort Laramie Treaty of 1851 paid an annuity to Indigenous nations and, in return, they gave up land around the migrant routes that crossed their territory.

b **EXAM QUESTION** Which of the following was the more important reason for the Fort Laramie Treaty of 1851:
- changes in US government policy
- changes in reasons for migration west?

Explain your answer with reference to **both** bullet points.

REVISION SKILLS

Reducing information to a more concise form is valuable. After reading a couple of pages of a textbook or your notes, ask yourself: 'What are the three most important things I need to remember?' Write those down on a piece of paper or small card. Don't worry about the things that you have left behind on the page; you'll remember those next time!

REVIEW

To refresh your memory about the Permanent Indian Frontier, look at page 24.

EXAMINER TIP

'Bullet point' questions will often ask you to think about things you have studied separately. It is advisable to spend some time looking at the notes you have made on early US government policy towards Indigenous nations (see page 24) before writing an answer to this question.

America 1840–1895 Expansion and Consolidation 27

The 'Indian Wars' (1862–1867)

The Colorado Gold Rush (1859–1863)

In 1858, gold was found in Pike's Peak, Colorado. During the Colorado Gold Rush, 100,000 migrants travelled through Cheyenne and Arapaho lands to reach Pike's Peak. The Fort Laramie Treaty of 1851 prohibited this, but the US government did not act. Meanwhile, migrants were demanding protection from Indigenous attacks.

'Exterminator' attitudes

Many Euro-Americans in the West believed that instead of negotiating with Indigenous nations, these nations should be removed to allow the USA to expand. They believed Indigenous people who resisted should be killed.

Indigenous leadership changes

Chiefs who had agreed to treaties lost influence when the US government did nothing about the migrants. Some bands, for example the Cheyenne Dog Soldiers, followed leaders who thought that war against Euro-Americans was now the best option for survival.

Reasons for the 'Indian Wars'

Settlement in Kansas and Nebraska

In 1854, Kansas and Nebraska were opened for settlement. US citizens could legally buy land in these new territories, even though the US government had agreed the land was Indigenous territory in the Fort Laramie Treaty of 1851.

The Civil War (1861–1865)

As the US Army left the West to fight the southern states, settler communities formed volunteer militias. These often had 'exterminator' views and launched murderous attacks on Indigenous bands.

The US government failed to pay annuities to some reservations because so much money was being spent fighting the southern states. For example, the Lower Sioux Reservation did not receive its annuity payment in 1862, and Indigenous people faced starvation.

The Sand Creek Massacre (1864)

On 29 November 1864, Colonel John Chivington and 675 men of the Colorado militia attacked a Cheyenne band led by chief Black Kettle. At least 150 Cheyenne people were killed and their bodies mutilated. This became known as the Sand Creek Massacre.

- The massacre happened during the Cheyenne War (1863–1867). The Cheyenne Dog Soldiers refused to accept a reservation treaty agreed by some Cheyenne chiefs. They resisted Euro-American migration through their lands.
- Black Kettle led a band that did not want to fight. He was promised protection if he and his band lived peacefully on the new reservation at Sand Creek.
- There were no Dog Soldiers at Sand Creek. The camp was made up of elders, women and children. These were the people the Colorado militia murdered.
- A US government investigation criticised Chivington, but he was not punished. After the massacre, Cheyenne bands allied with Lakota bands under Red Cloud.

Red Cloud's War (1866–1868) and Fetterman's Trap (1866)

- In 1862, prospectors found gold in Montana. The Bozeman Trail was a short cut to the goldfields. It crossed Lakota hunting grounds, against the Fort Laramie Treaty of 1851.
- In 1866, the US Army wanted to negotiate safe travel along the Bozeman Trail for migrants. Lakota chief Red Cloud discovered 700 soldiers in the area without permission from the Lakota. He led the Lakota, Cheyenne and Arapaho in a war against the USA.
- Fetterman's Trap was a key event during Red Cloud's War. Captain William Fetterman and 81 soldiers were tricked into riding out after a small Lakota raiding party. They were then killed in an ambush by around 1,000 warriors.

The consequences of the 'Indian Wars'

Red Cloud won his war against the US Army. As a result, the US government was forced to negotiate a new treaty: the Fort Laramie Treaty of 1868.

- The Bozeman Trail was closed and three forts built by the US Army were demolished.
- The Great Sioux Reservation (an area of 48,000 square miles) was guaranteed for the Oceti Sakowin forever. This area included the sacred Paha Sapa (Black Hills).
- Except for authorised government officials, no one apart from Indigenous people was permitted to enter the Great Sioux Reservation.
- In return, the Oceti Sakowin and its allies would remain at peace with the USA and its citizens.

SOURCE A *Photo of Red Cloud c1875. Red Cloud chose to be photographed as a diplomat: he is holding a peace pipe in one hand and a treaty in the other.*

SUMMARY

- The first Fort Laramie Treaty of 1851 was designed to stop migrant settlers crossing Indigenous territory.
- Many Euro-American migrant settlers had an 'exterminator' attitude; they believed Indigenous people who resisted should be killed. Colonel John Chivington was not punished after the Sand Creek Massacre (1864).
- The second Fort Laramie Treaty of 1868 followed the US Army's defeat by Red Cloud. The USA agreed to Red Cloud's demands.

APPLY

BULLET POINTS

a Make connections between the following points and the 'Indian Wars'.
- The Civil War meant the US Army needed its soldiers in the South.
- Settlers in the West who feared Indigenous attacks formed militias.
- Gold was found in Colorado in 1858 and in Montana in 1862.

b Which of the following was the more important reason for the 'Indian Wars':
- the Civil War
- gold rushes?

Explain your answer with reference to **both** bullet points.

EXAMINER TIP

Do not spend time writing down everything you know about the Civil War or gold rushes. Focus on the Civil War and the gold rushes as *reasons* for the 'Indian Wars'.

CHAPTER 5

The American Civil War (1861–1865)

RECAP

The background to the Civil War

There were significant differences between the North and South of the USA. These differences created tensions that were kept in check for a long time but, after Abraham Lincoln was elected President in 1860, southern states began to **secede** from the USA. They formed the **Confederacy**. The states remaining in the USA became known as the Union. The Civil War began soon afterwards, in April 1861.

The expansion of the USA

Compromises were made to keep a balance of slave states (which supported slavery) and free states (which supported the abolition of slavery) as the USA expanded. A balance of slave states and free states meant a balance of political power in **federal government**.

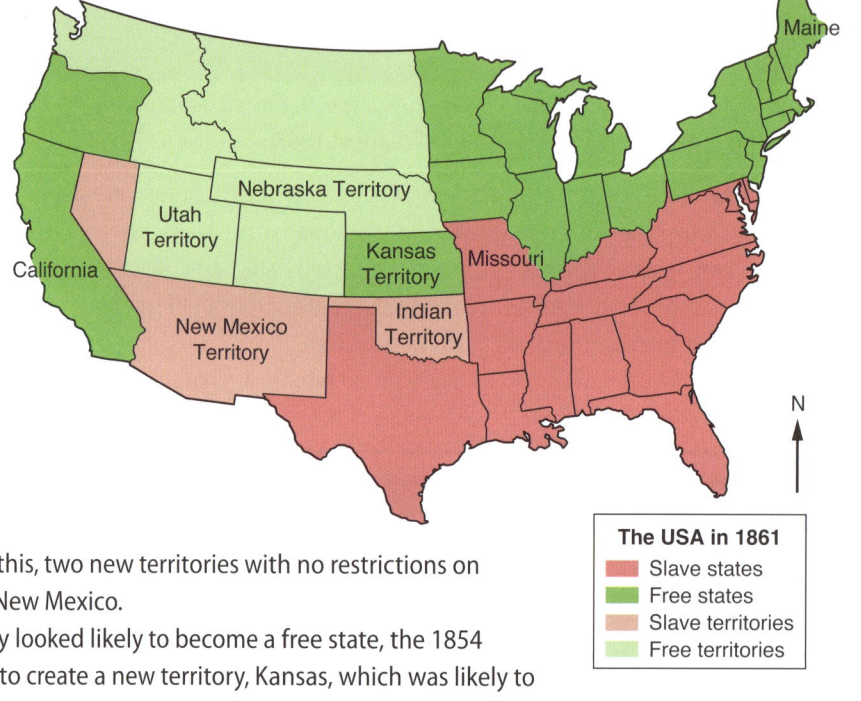

The USA in 1861
- Slave states
- Free states
- Slave territories
- Free territories

- In 1820, the Missouri Compromise made Maine a free state to balance Missouri as a slave state.
- In 1850, California became a free state. To balance this, two new territories with no restrictions on slavery were created: Utah and New Mexico.
- In 1854, when Nebraska Territory looked likely to become a free state, the 1854 Kansas–Nebraska Act divided it to create a new territory, Kansas, which was likely to become a slave state.
- However, opposition to slavery in Kansas increased as thousands moved there from the North. **Abolitionist** John Brown attacked pro-slavery settlers, increasing tensions.

Tariffs

Many in southern states argued that **tariffs** benefitted the North but harmed the South.

- Tariffs protected the North's manufacturing industries by making imported products more expensive than US-made products.
- In response, countries like Britain brought in their own tariffs. The South sold most of its cotton to Britain. Now the South sold less cotton abroad because tariffs made it too expensive.

Abolition fears

Many in the South became convinced that northern politicians wanted to abolish slavery everywhere in the USA. They were worried because the economy of the South relied on the labour of enslaved people to grow cotton.

- In 1859, John Brown led a failed attempt to start a revolt by enslaved people in Virginia. There was a lot of support for Brown's illegal actions in the North, which alarmed southern politicians and slaveholders.
- In 1860, Abraham Lincoln was elected president. Even though Lincoln said he would not get rid of slavery in states where it already existed, many in the South believed he planned to abolish it throughout the USA.

APPLY

INTERPRETATION ANALYSIS

a   Read **Interpretation A** and **Interpretation B** about the tensions that led to the Civil War and then copy and complete the following table.

	Interpretation A	Interpretation B
Who is the author of the interpretation?		
When was the interpretation written?		
Why was the interpretation written?		
What does the interpretation say was the main tension that led to the Civil War?		

▼ **INTERPRETATION A** *Adapted from a letter from Stephen F. Hale to the Governor of Kentucky, written in December 1860. Hale was a 'secession commissioner', appointed by the state of Alabama to make links with Kentucky about its plans to leave the Union:*

> A quarter of a century ago, the Northern States began waging an unrelenting and fanatical war on the institution of African slavery in the Southern States. This African slavery, worth $4 billion, has long supported the economy of most of the Southern States, supplied the world with its most valuable trade and provided the manufacturing industries of North America and Europe with their raw material and their workers with the money to feed their families.
>
> Will the South give up the institution of slavery, and agree that her citizens be stripped of their property, her civilization destroyed, the whole land laid waste by fire and sword? It is impossible; disunion is inevitable.

▼ **INTERPRETATION B** *Adapted from* The Rise and Fall of the Confederate Government *by Jefferson Davis, published in 1881. Jefferson Davis was the president of the Confederate States of America during the Civil War. After the war he was put in prison but then released without trial. He wrote this book to justify the reasons for secession and for his actions during the war:*

> Slavery was not the cause of the conflict. The Southern States and the Southern people are consistently represented as 'propagandists' for slavery, and the Northern States and people as the defenders and champions of universal freedom. But these representations are false. While slavery was a factor in the conflict, it was not the cause. The cause was not the raid of John Brown, it was not the unjust and unequal tariff laws. It was the systematic and persistent struggle of the North to deprive the Southern States of equality in the Union, excluding them from the new Territories which are the common property of all the States.

b
   1. How does **Interpretation B** differ from **Interpretation A** about the tensions that led to the Civil War?
   2. Why might the authors of **Interpretations A** and **B** have a different interpretation about the tensions that led to the Civil War?
   3. Which interpretation gives the more convincing explanation about the tensions that led to the Civil War?

> **EXAMINER TIP**
>
> For Question 2, the time at which the authors are writing may be important as a difference, or the reason why they were writing, or the audience they were writing for.

> **EXAMINER TIP**
>
> For Question 3, you need to support your decision about which interpretation is more convincing using your own contextual knowledge to evaluate each interpretation. Don't repeat points about provenance from Question 2 here, as they won't get you any marks.

 **RECAP**

The impacts of the Civil War

Around 750,000 men were killed fighting in the Civil War. The war also had enormous social and economic consequences for civilians (non-military people) in both the North and the South.

The lives of Black American civilians during the war

Changes	However…
There were many more jobs for Black people in northern cities, as so many white men had joined the armed forces to fight. Many freed Black Americans from the South also moved North to find jobs in northern cities and factories.	White workers attacked Black workers, and burned Black people's homes and businesses, complaining that Black people were taking 'their' jobs. In northern cities, Black workers generally experienced worse living and working conditions than white workers.
In 1863, President Lincoln declared the **Emancipation** of all enslaved people in Confederate states. Enslaved people knew that, if they could reach Union forces in the South, they would be free.	Emancipation made no difference to most enslaved people *during the war* because they were in areas that were still controlled by the Confederacy.
400,000 acres of land in Georgia and South Carolina were confiscated from **plantation** owners and given to freed Black families in 40-acre plots for them to farm themselves.	After the war, the Black families who had been given 40-acre plots had to give them back to plantation owners.

Other social and economic changes experienced by civilians

Conscription

Both sides introduced conscription during the war. The South made people serve in the military rather than relying on volunteers in 1862, and the North in 1863. Conscription was unpopular. In the North, there were riots against conscription, and thousands travelled to Canada to escape it.

Shortages

Trade between the North and the South stopped during the Civil War. Civilians in the North couldn't get southern products like cotton, sugar and tobacco. However, shortages were worse in the South, which imported most of its products. This was because the North blocked southern ports: called a blockade.

Inflation

During the Civil War, both sides spent over $3 billion supplying their armed forces, and both sides printed more money to help pay for the war. This, together with the shortages, caused high **inflation**. Inflation was much worse in the South because shortages were worse. There, prices increased by 9,000 per cent! The Confederate currency became almost worthless. People had to barter (swap) things they had for things they needed, which meant people could not always be certain whether they could get food, clothing, medicine and other necessities of life.

Work in the countryside

Women, older people and children had to take on men's roles in farming. In the South, enslaved people did most of the work, but when Union forces came near, many enslaved people went to them to become free. As a result, many farms and plantations were abandoned because of the shortage of workers.

Work in cities

Army pay was better than low-paid factory work, so many men in northern cities joined the army. Women took up some of the poorly paid factory jobs they left behind. This included working in munitions factories making shells and bullets.

SUMMARY

- The causes of the Civil War went back many years and were based on differences between North and South. Slavery was at the heart of the conflict.
- In 1863, President Lincoln declared the Emancipation of all enslaved people in the USA. The Confederacy refused to accept this.
- The Civil War had enormous economic and social impacts on civilians on both sides.

APPLY

IN WHAT WAYS

a How did the following cause problems to civilians during the Civil War:
- conscription
- shortages and inflation?

b Copy and complete the following table.

Groups of civilians	Economic impacts of the Civil War	Social impacts of the Civil War
Black Americans in the South		
Black Americans in the North		
White Americans in the South		
White Americans in the North		

c **EXAM QUESTION** In what ways were the lives of civilians affected by the Civil War (1861–c1865)?

EXAMINER TIP

You must write about two or more ways that people's lives were affected. You could write about two different ways the same group of people were affected, or you could write about two different groups of people.

America 1840–1895 Expansion and Consolidation 33

CHAPTER 6 The aftermath of the Civil War

RECAP

The economic impacts of the Civil War

Industrialisation increased rapidly in the USA after the Civil War ended in April 1865, but the North benefitted most from this economic growth.

New taxes introduced to pay for the war continued after 1865, and the money was used to help the US economy, especially in the South. However, the taxes were unpopular and were stopped by 1872.

Economic growth meant lots of jobs were created, which attracted immigrants from Europe. However, this led to anti-immigrant tensions.

The transcontinental railroad connected farming and mining in the West with the industries of the northern cities.

New federal banking rules and paper money increased investment in northern industries, creating thousands of new jobs.

Consequences for the North

Consequences for the South

Cotton remained the South's main export, but after the war cotton prices fell because other countries started selling cotton. The 11 ex-Confederate states remained the poorest part of the USA for the next 100 years.

Euro-Americans in the South generally refused to accept Black Americans as equals. Discrimination and persecution of Black people continued.

White people's incomes fell by 40 per cent in the South after the war. **Freedpeople's** incomes went up, but then they hadn't earned anything before the war.

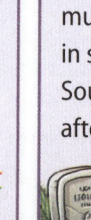

With 75,000–100,000 Confederate soldiers killed during the war, there were fewer people to farm the land, and as much as a third of land in some areas of the South wasn't farmed after the war.

34 Chapter 6 The aftermath of the Civil War

52–57 Revision progress

Amendments to the US Constitution

The Thirteenth Amendment and the Black Codes

In 1863, Emancipation abolished slavery in Confederate states only. The Thirteenth Amendment (December 1865) abolished slavery everywhere in the USA.

The southern states responded by developing the 'Black Codes', laws that aimed to control freedpeople and keep them dependent on their employers, in a similar way to slavery. For example:

- South Carolina: Black people could only get jobs in agriculture or as domestic servants.
- Texas: if a freedman quit his job without permission, he lost all his wages.
- Florida: if Black men did not have a job, they were arrested and the state could hire them out to work for a year.

The Civil Rights Act and the Fourteenth Amendment

The Civil Rights Act (1866) said that everyone born in the USA was a US citizen and that all US citizens had the same rights. (Indigenous people were not included.) States were not allowed to make laws that restricted these rights in any way.

Because a future **Congress** might repeal the Civil Rights Act or change it, the Fourteenth Amendment (1868) made equal rights for all US citizens a part of the US Constitution.

 APPLY

INTERPRETATION ANALYSIS

Read this interpretation.

▼ **INTERPRETATION A** *Adapted from a speech by Daniel Ullmann, made in New York City in 1868. During the Civil War, President Lincoln asked Ullmann, a white officer, to organise the first Black regiments from men who had escaped enslavement in Louisiana:*

> For hundreds of years Black people of the South have stood firm. They were born here and have been full of hopes and fears, their destinies tightly woven together with that of this nation. Yet, they have been degraded and regarded as ignorant. Despite this, when the Civil War began they stood with the Union. We must give them the right to vote. This right should be automatically granted to all US citizens; it is not a privilege.

a Which side did Daniel Ullmann fight for during the Civil War?
b How might Daniel Ullmann's experiences leading Black regiments have influenced his views?
c What view does Daniel Ullmann have about civil rights for Black Americans?

REVISION SKILLS

Some students think that you can't revise for 'interpretation' questions because you won't see the interpretations until the exam. This isn't the case! You can practise identifying what interpretations are saying about an event or issue, and comparing that with your own knowledge. And you can practise analysing the provenance (caption) to explain reasons for differences.

America 1840–1895 Expansion and Consolidation 35

 **RECAP**

Reconstruction

The challenges of Reconstruction

President Andrew Johnson faced challenges from **Radical Republicans**, who dominated Congress, about how **Reconstruction** (rebuilding and re-establishing the southern states after the Civil War) should happen. For example:

- Johnson wanted 10 per cent of voters to swear loyalty to the Union before states could rejoin the USA. Radical Republicans wanted 50 per cent.
- Johnson thought Black Americans should be given the vote gradually, starting with **veterans**. Radical Republicans wanted freedmen to get the vote immediately.

The impacts of Reconstruction

Despite opposition from President Johnson, Congress passed the Reconstruction Act in 1867, which put each ex-Confederate state under military control until it had voted in a new constitution and approved the Thirteenth and Fourteenth Amendments. Then the state could send representatives to Congress and govern itself again.

Black voting rights	Opposition to Black voting rights
Equal civil rights includes equal voting rights. There were almost 4 million Black citizens in the South and they used their votes to make changes: • Two Black senators were elected in 1870 and 1875. • Thousands of Black people were elected to state government positions. • Black representation made sure new state constitutions that supported the Thirteenth and Fourteenth Amendments were passed.	There was strong opposition to Black voting rights, Black people in state government and the new state constitutions among white southerners. • The Ku Klux Klan and other **white supremacist** organisations were formed to stop Black people voting, by using violence and intimidation. • The US government tried to stop this terrorism but, as one group was suppressed, others sprang up. • By the end of Reconstruction, in 1877, white southerners controlled state government again.

The Freedmen's Bureau	Opposition to the Freedmen's Bureau
In 1865, the US government set up the Freedmen's Bureau. • The Freedmen's Bureau helped people freed from slavery and also white families experiencing poverty. For example, it provided food and clothing, as well as legal advice about work contracts. • When asked, freedpeople most wanted help with education. By 1870, over 1,000 schools had been set up by freedpeople, some with help from the Freedmen's Bureau.	In 1872, the US government shut down the Freedmen's Bureau because it was causing too much conflict. • The Bureau's programmes cost a lot of money, which meant taxes went up, which is often unpopular. • Some southerners resented '**carpetbaggers**', people from the North who they said used Reconstruction to make themselves rich and powerful through corruption and swindling. • White supremacists attacked freedpeople's schools and teachers: over 600 schools were attacked between 1865 and 1876.

The balance of federal and state powers

President Johnson believed that the federal government should interfere as little as possible in the right of states to govern themselves. The Radical Republicans disagreed: they believed federal government should step in if states tried to take away rights given to everyone living in the country. At the beginning of Reconstruction federal power was strong but, by the end of Reconstruction, states were more powerful.

SUMMARY

- The economic consequences of the Civil War benefitted the North but not the South.
- Reconstruction aimed to reunite the USA, but attempts by the federal government to give freedpeople the same rights as Euro-Americans met with very strong opposition.
- By the end of Reconstruction, white southern governments had deprived Black Americans of many of their rights as US citizens.

 **APPLY**

INTERPRETATION ANALYSIS

Read this interpretation.

▼ **INTERPRETATION A** *Adapted from an interview given by Emma Falconer for a US folklore project in 1936. Emma Falconer was 15 years old and living in Texas at the start of Reconstruction. Texas had been part of the Confederacy during the Civil War. The interpretation uses racist language:*

> The negroes had been set free and were supported by the office of the 'freedmen's bureau'. Many left the plantation on which they were born and went to the cities expecting the freedmen's bureau to feed and clothe them so they did not have to work, but this body could not care for all. Therefore, stealing and arson took place.
>
> We all know how carpetbaggers, unprincipled politicians from the North, came down and took charge and deprived the whites who fought in the rebel army from voting and the many offices were given to the former slaves or their offspring. There is no doubt that the indignities that were heaped on the south led to acts of retaliation. The Ku Klux Klan was intended to restore order, as well as a protection to the communities which were suffering from these troubles.

a In your own words, explain why Falconer is critical of the Freedmen's Bureau.

b What do you know about the Freedmen's Bureau that agrees or disagrees with Falconer's interpretation?

c Do you agree or disagree with Falconer's interpretation of the Ku Klux Klan? Explain your answer using your contextual knowledge.

BULLET POINTS

a Imagine you are each of these people and write a paragraph explaining your view:
  - A Radical Republican who supports the Fourteenth Amendment.
  - President Johnson, who opposes the Fourteenth Amendment.

b Which of the following was the more important reason for the Fourteenth Amendment:
  - the Black Codes
  - Radical Republicans?

  Explain your answer with reference to **both** bullet points.

EXAMINER TIP

There are 12 marks available for the 'bullet points' question, which means you should spend around 15 minutes on your answer. Use a couple of these minutes to quickly plan the points you want to make.

Chapter 7: Continued settlement of the West

The Homestead Act (1862)

The background to the Homestead Act (1862)

- By the 1860s, the US government was under a lot of pressure to open up the Plains for settlement as land prices rose in the East and Far West. There was high demand for land.

- **Homesteaders** (family farmers) wanted Indigenous nations to be moved out of the way, and they wanted legal title to 'their' land so no one could take it away from them.

- The US government used treaties to move Plains nations onto reservations. They then divided up the land they had obtained into 640-acre sections and put these up for sale at around $1 per acre. Buyers would get legal title to the land.

- However, around $1 per acre was too expensive for most people: $640 was a year's wages for most workers. As a result, there were campaigns to make land on the Plains more affordable.

Features of the Homestead Act (1862)

President Lincoln passed the Homestead Act in 1862, after secession in 1861 removed southern opposition to such an act.

The Homestead Act deliberately made it easy for a wide range of people to file a claim and get legal title to their land after living on the land and farming it for five years.

Features of the Homestead Act (1862)

Requirements

Who could file a claim?
- Head of a household or at least 21 years old
- Citizen or intending to become a citizen

What did they have to do?
- Pay a small filing fee ($12)
- Build a home on the land
- Farm the land for at least five years
- Pay a 'proving up' fee to gain legal title ($6)

Successes — Lots of claims!
- 4 million claims in total
- Union Army veterans only had to live on their homestead for a year before they could 'prove up'
- Attractive to immigrants, who didn't need to be US citizens to file a claim

Amendments — Timber Culture Act (1873)
- Added 160 acres if the homesteader planted trees on 40 acres of the original plot

Criticisms

Indigenous dispossession
- Indigenous nations were made to give up their land for settlers to claim.
- This often went against previous treaties guaranteeing their lands.

High rate of failure
- 60 per cent of homesteaders didn't 'prove up' and gave up their homesteads.
- Although the land was cheap, farmers needed serious money to succeed.

Speculation
- The government failed to prevent rich people from making lots of claims.
- This land was then sold on for profit.

160 acres was too small
- In drier and in colder parts of the Plains, 160 acres was too small for a farm.
- Many homestead farms included unproductive land within the 160 acres.

Why did southern states oppose the Homestead Act?

Republicans wanted the Plains to be settled by homesteaders rather than by big businesses or southern plantation-style farming. The Republicans knew that homesteaders would vote for them and strengthen their position in Congress.

Southern states blocked attempts to make land affordable because they knew more homesteaders would mean more free states (as homesteader farms wouldn't be able to sell crops as cheaply as the plantations that used enslaved labour). An increase in free states would weaken the South in Congress.

APPLY

INTERPRETATION ANALYSIS

Read this interpretation.

▼ **INTERPRETATION A** *Adapted from an interview with Albert Reed for a project about the settlement of Oklahoma in 1938. Albert Reed married in 1882 and the newly-weds migrated to Kansas soon after, before moving again to a homestead in Oklahoma in 1892:*

> As time went on, merchants and farm implement dealers pressed the farmers to mortgage their land to buy horses, implements, and other improvements. This led to much unwise buying and mortgaging and in the end many settlers were driven from their farms by foreclosures*. Many times a farmer bought a full line of farm implements and did not get them paid for before they had to be replaced. Cases were frequent when every horse, cow, hog and chicken on the place was mortgaged.
>
> * A 'foreclosure' is when a lender (such as a bank) recovers at least some of the money it has loaned to someone by seizing their possessions, including land, selling them and keeping the money.

a   Explain the problem that Albert Reed describes here in your own words.
b   Why were homestead farmers particularly likely to suffer from this problem?
c   How do you think this problem related to the high failure rate of homesteads on the Plains?

DESCRIBE

a   Write brief answers to the following questions:
   • How was homestead farming different from plantation farming?
   • Why didn't southern states want a Homestead Act?
   • Why did settlers want to pay for land rather than just start farming public land (land owned by the federal government) for free?
   • Why was it much easier for the US government to pass a Homestead Act in 1862 than in 1860?
b   Was the Homestead Act a success or a failure? Include one reason why the US government could consider it a success, and one reason why it could be considered a failure in your answer.
c   **EXAM QUESTION** Describe two problems faced by the US government when settling the Plains.

EXAMINER TIP
Aim to write about the same amount for each of the problems you describe.

 RECAP

The Pacific Railroad Act (1862)

Features of the Pacific Railroad Act (1862)

Union Pacific and Central Pacific
- The Act made it possible for the Union Pacific Railroad Company and the Central Pacific Railroad Company to build the first transcontinental railroad.
- Immigrants played a vital role: over 8,000 Irish, German and Italian labourers built the Union Pacific line, and over 10,000 Chinese labourers built the Central Pacific line.

Public money
- The government loaned the two companies $16,000 for every mile of track they built ($48,000 per mile in the mountains).

Features of the Pacific Railroad Act of 1862

Land grants
- The US government also gave the two companies 10 square miles of land for every mile of track they built, which the companies sold.
- This land was laid out in a 'checkerboard' pattern, with 1-square-mile sections of public land alternating with 1-square-mile sections of railroad land.

Indigenous rights
- The first transcontinental railroad went through land that treaties stated belonged to Indigenous nations.
- In order to grant millions of acres of land to the railroad companies, new treaties were made that 'extinguished' Indigenous rights to the land and pushed Indigenous people onto reservations.
- When nations resisted, the US Army guarded railroad workers, attacked Indigenous communities and destroyed bison herds. It even encouraged Euro-Americans to visit the Plains to kill as many bison as possible.

Railroads and settlement of the Plains

The US government giving public land to the transcontinental railroad companies played a very important role in settling the Plains.

- By 1880, the railroad companies had sold 200 million acres in the West for settlement.
- In comparison, by 1884, only 13 million acres of land had been 'proved up' by homesteaders.

People bought railroad land because:

- the railroad companies ran huge campaigns to persuade people to buy their land, including marketing campaigns in European countries
- farmers could send crops to markets in the East and the Far West by rail, and order new machinery from the East to tackle the problems of farming the Plains.

Transcontinental railroads also made it easier for settlers to reach the Plains. They no longer had to a make the time-consuming and dangerous trip by wagon.

APPLY

INTERPRETATION ANALYSIS

Read **Interpretation A**.

▼ **INTERPRETATION A** *Adapted from* Our Indian Wards *by George Manypenny, published in 1880. Manypenny was Commissioner for Indian Affairs between 1853 and 1857. In later years he argued that the USA should start treating Indigenous nations with justice and fairness:*

> In 1866, treaties were made with the Cherokees, Choctaws, Chickasaws, and Creeks which gave corporations the right to construct railroads through their territories. But a clause was also added that was dangerous to their interests and their peace in the future. This was the clause that provided land for the railroad corporation of every alternate section of land along the railroad line. Following this, there were discussions in Congress about using these land grants to open reservations to the occupation and settlement of the white people – even though the Indians had the government's guarantee in law that the country they now own, which they were given in return for their homes east of the Mississippi, should be their permanent home forever.

a The first transcontinental railroad was completed in 1869. What does **Interpretation A** tell you about its impacts?

b What can you identify in **Interpretation A** that agrees with anything you already know about the construction of railroads on the Plains?

c What do you already know about the Cherokees? How does that fit with what you read in **Interpretation A**? (Hint: Indian Removal Act)

d How convincing do you find **Interpretation A** about the impacts of the railroads on Indigenous nations?

Now read **Interpretation B**.

▼ **INTERPRETATION B** *Adapted from* When Railroads Were New *by Charles F. Carter, published in 1909. Charles Carter is described as 'an old railroad man':*

> The completion of the Pacific railroads did more than anything else to put an end to organized outlawry in the West, and to curb hostile Indians, who up to that time had cost the government one hundred thousand dollars each to kill. It developed a trade which earned for the Central Pacific alone, in the first three months, $1,703,000. Also, the construction of the Union Pacific netted its builders the neat profit of $16,710,432, or twenty-seven per cent on the cost.

e **EXAM QUESTION** Which interpretation gives the more convincing opinion about the impacts of the first transcontinental railroad? Explain your answer based on your contextual knowledge and what it says in **Interpretations A** and **B**.

> **REVIEW**
>
> Look back at page 24 for more on early US government policy towards Indigenous nations.

> **EXAMINER TIP**
>
> Consider what you already know that supports or contradicts statements made in both the interpretations.

Farming the Plains

The problems of farming the Plains

Homesteading was based on farming crops. But the grasslands of the Plains were not suitable for European-style crop farming.

The **sod** broke cast-iron ploughs. Farmers had to dig by hand, which was exhausting. They could hire professional 'sod-busters', but this was expensive.

Dry summers meant the long grass on the Plains burned easily. Fires spread quickly and burned everything in their path.

Problems associated with farming the Plains

The Plains environment was too dry for trees to grow, and homesteaders had to import wood for fences, tools, fuel and homes, which was expensive.

Filing a claim was cheap, but homesteaders needed around $1,000 to buy everything they needed to begin farming (around two years' wages). Most took out bank loans, which charged high rates of interest.

Solutions for farming problems

The industrialisation of the USA from the middle of the nineteenth century meant solutions to the problems associated with farming the Plains began to be developed. However, it was decades before improved technology was widely used, and its use led to terrible environmental problems by the 1930s.

John Deere developed a strong steel plough in 1837, which could break up the sod. However, it was very expensive. In the 1860s, James Oliver's improvements made the steel plough more effective and affordable.

Dry farming techniques were developed to trap water in the soil. More powerful well drillers that could reach water 150m underground were also developed. And then self-governing windmills were invented in 1854, to pump the water to the surface.

Solving the problems associated with farming the Plains

Homesteaders built houses using sods for bricks. Others got around the lack of wood on the Plains by digging dugout homes. Protecting crops from cattle or wild animals with fences became much easier after Joseph Glidden invented barbed wire in 1874.

If homesteaders could not pay back the money they had borrowed, the bank took their farms. These people often then became workers for more successful farmers. Hiring more workers meant successful farmers could expand.

42 Chapter 7 Continued settlement of the West

The Plains received very little rainfall and were very cold in the winter. Crops that grew well elsewhere shrivelled and died on the Plains.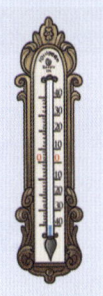

Most areas of the Plains had no rivers. This meant many farmers couldn't water their crops.

Swarms of grasshoppers that ate crops were common. In Nebraska in 1874, approximately 120 billion insects devastated over 115,800 square miles of land.

Farmers found crops that grew well in dry conditions, such as Turkey Red wheat. Other types of wheat were also found that could be planted in spring, when soils had the most moisture, and harvested before winter, avoiding the very low temperatures.

Natural disasters, such as fires and insects, were difficult to deal with. The homesteaders had to protect their crops as best they could by, for example, harvesting crops before grasshoppers arrived.

SUMMARY

- The Homestead Act of 1862 made it affordable for most Americans to own a 160-acre homestead on the Plains.
- However, following the Pacific Railroad Act of 1862, railroad companies were responsible for more settlement of the Plains in the nineteenth century.
- The Plains were not suitable for European-style crop farming, and homesteaders faced many problems.
- Over time, solutions were developed that enabled the Plains to be farmed successfully, but in a way that led to terrible environmental problems in the 1930s.

APPLY

BULLET POINTS

a Explain how the following inventions helped solve the problems associated with farming the Plains:
- John Deere's steel plough
- Joseph Glidden's barbed wire.

b How did railroads help farmers on the Plains?

c Which of the following was the more important reason for successful farming on the Plains:
- transcontinental railroads
- agricultural inventions?

Explain your answer with reference to **both** bullet points.

EXAMINER TIP

Remember to back up the points you make with evidence (such as the names of inventions and inventors) and explain how they were reasons for successful farming on the Plains.

REVIEW

Look back at pages 40 and 41 to remind yourself of the impact of railroads on the Plains.

America 1840–1895 Expansion and Consolidation 43

CHAPTER 8 Indigenous resistance

RECAP

President Grant's Peace Policy

Reasons for President Grant's Peace Policy

Ulysses S. Grant became US president in 1869 and announced a new policy towards Indigenous peoples in his first speech. He said he wanted to build a peaceful relationship by removing the following four causes of conflict between the USA and Indigenous peoples.

1 Corruption in reservation administration
Reservations were often run by corrupt Indian agents who held back annuities and food rations. When, or if, food supplies did arrive, they were sometimes terrible quality. Some agents used starvation as a way of controlling Indigenous people.

2 US government failures
The US government had not stopped Euro-Americans settling on reservation land. The US government also withheld annuity payments or was sometimes late making annuity payments, which meant Indigenous people suffered and lost trust in the US government.

3 Indigenous people's hunting practices
The old reservations policy tried to persuade Indigenous people to stop hunting and start farming. But Indigenous nations continued to hunt if their reservations were large enough to support enough animals, or left their reservations to return to old hunting grounds.

4 Treaties and sovereign nations
Grant said that Indigenous nations were not strong enough to be called 'sovereign', because their leaders were not able to stop their people from breaking treaties. Therefore, making treaties with Indigenous people was a mistake.

The aims of President Grant's Peace Policy

The Peace Policy aimed to resolve the four causes of conflict.

1 Corruption in reservation administration *SOLUTION*
Christian Churches should run reservations and missionaries should act as Indian agents. This would ensure high moral standards, and an end to corruption and theft.

2 US government failures *SOLUTION*
Reservations must be supplied properly, so people received weekly rations and did not become desperate from hunger. US Army forts would stop settlers taking any more reservation land (and also stop Indigenous people leaving reservations). However, the government would hold on to annuity money for Indigenous nations and use it to pay for what the government decided they needed.

3 Indigenous people's hunting practices *SOLUTION*
Indigenous people should be forced to farm by making reservations smaller. Larger reservations encouraged Indigenous bands to continue hunting, but there were limited opportunities to hunt on smaller reservations. The US Army was also instructed to reduce bison numbers: without bison, horse nations would have to stay in one place and grow food.

4 Treaties and sovereign nations *SOLUTION*
In 1871, the US government decided that no new treaties would be made and that Indigenous people were now **wards** of the federal government, not members of independent nations. It became the federal government's responsibility to make sure Indigenous people **assimilated** into US society.

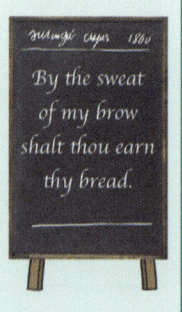

INTERPRETATION ANALYSIS

Read this interpretation.

▼ **INTERPRETATION A**   *Adapted from 'The White Earth Reservation', published in the* Tomahawk *newspaper in 1903. This newspaper was published by members of the White Earth Reservation, an Ojibwe (Chippewa) reservation in Minnesota. The newspaper frequently challenged the actions of the Bureau of Indian Affairs:*

> The first Indian agent that was appointed under President Grant's famous peace policy was E.P. Smith. Immediately after Mr Smith took charge of the White Earth Indian agency in 1871, he succeeded in convincing a large number of Indians to move to the reservation; and, by his policy of dealing with and encouraging them, persuaded more Indians to start farming than all the agents here have since succeeded in doing. While the progress of the Indians as farmers has been very slow and unsatisfactory to the government, there are a great many of the members of this reservation who have from 100 to 500 acres of land under cultivation on their farms.

a   Make a note of the actions that **Interpretation A** says the Indian agent took when he was appointed to the White Earth Reservation.

b   How well do the actions you've noted down fit with what you know about the aims of President Grant's Peace Policy?

c   What impression do you get of how the author of the article felt about E.P. Smith? Write down a quote from the interpretation that shows this.

REVISION SKILLS

History is as much about how you use the knowledge you have as it is about what you know. Practise reading interpretations, identifying their point of view and coming up with evidence that either supports or argues against their view.

DESCRIBE

a   Outline President Grant's solutions to the following problems with the US government's reservation policy:
   - corruption by Indian agents
   - settlers taking reservation land for themselves
   - lack of food on reservations
   - Indigenous bands not following agreements set out in treaties.

b   **EXAM QUESTION** Describe two problems President Grant attempted to solve with his Peace Policy.

 **RECAP**

Euro-American attitudes to Indigenous people

The 'Indian problem'

In the nineteenth century, Euro-Americans talked of the 'Indian problem': what should be done about Indigenous nations. There were two main attitudes, and both are considered racist today.

> 'Exterminators' believed that Indigenous people should be moved out of the way if they 'interfered with progress' (if US citizens wanted their land). They called Indigenous people 'savages' and thought military force should be used to stamp out any sign of resistance.

> 'Humanitarians' believed that the 'march of progress' made it, sadly, inevitable that the Indigenous way of life would disappear. Their answer to the 'Indian problem' was assimilation. They saw Indigenous people as children who had to be taught to behave in a 'civilised' way, and disciplined severely if they did not learn.

President Grant's Peace Policy was based on 'humanitarian' views: Indigenous people were wards who should be guided towards 'civilisation' and citizenship. However, Grant was prepared to use 'exterminator' methods to achieve his aims.

Protecting the railroads

- In 1869, Grant put General Sherman in charge of protecting the transcontinental railroad workers from attacks by Indigenous bands, who were angry that – despite treaty agreements – they were being made to give up their land.
- Sherman's troops destroyed Indigenous crops, killed the horses the bands used for transport, burned down their camps during winter (when it was much harder for people to find food and shelter), and destroyed all the hunting weapons they found.
- These strategies forced bands to choose between starvation or moving onto reservations.

The extermination of the bison

The great bison herds were systematically exterminated as part of the Peace Policy.

- The completion of the first transcontinental railroad in 1869 brought thousands of hunters to the Plains.
- By the 1880s, Indigenous bands could find no bison to hunt at all, forcing them to choose between starvation or moving onto reservations.

46 Chapter 8 Indigenous resistance

APPLY

INTERPRETATION ANALYSIS

Read **Interpretation A** and **Interpretation B**.

▼ **INTERPRETATION A** *Adapted from* A Lady's Life in the Rocky Mountains *by Isabella Bird, published in 1879. Isabella Bird was a British explorer who visited the Rocky Mountains in 1873:*

> The Americans will never solve the Indian problem till the Indian is extinct. The way they treat them as enemies has intensified their treachery and 'devilry'. The way they treat them as friends reduces them to a degraded pauperism [poverty], without even the first signs of civilisation. The Indian Agency is full of fraud and corruption. It is said that barely thirty per cent of annuities ever reaches the reservations; and the complaints of shoddy blankets, damaged flour, and worthless firearms are universal. 'To get rid of the Injuns' is the phrase used everywhere. If gold is found on their reservations, then those reservations get 'rushed', and their possessors are either compelled to accept land farther west or are shot or driven off.

▼ **INTERPRETATION B** *Adapted from* The Indian Problem *by Nelson Miles, published in 1879. Nelson Miles was a US Army general who had a leading role in the army's campaigns against Indigenous nations. Here he reflects on US government policy in the early 1870s:*

> Why has our management of Indian affairs been less successful than that of Canada? It can be answered in a few words. Their system is permanent, decided, and just, and ours is not. The tide of immigration in Canada has not been as great as along our frontier. They have been able to allow the Indians to live as Indians, which we have not, and do not attempt to force upon them the customs which are distasteful to them.

a In **Interpretation A**, Isabella Bird talks about treating Indigenous people as enemies and as friends.

Explain what she says are the results of these two approaches.

b Why does Nelson Miles say Canada has been more successful at dealing with the 'Indian problem' than the USA? Use quotes from **Interpretation B** to back up your answer.

c Which author do you think was best placed to understand the 'Indian problem', Isabella Bird or Nelson Miles? Use the information provided about the provenance of the interpretations to help you answer this question.

d
1. How does **Interpretation B** differ from **Interpretation A** about how to deal with the 'Indian problem'? Explain your answer using **Interpretations A** and **B**.

2. Why might the authors of **Interpretations A** and **B** have a different interpretation about how to deal with the 'Indian problem'? Explain your answer using **Interpretations A** and **B** and your contextual knowledge.

3. Which interpretation gives the more convincing opinion about how to deal with the 'Indian problem'? Explain your answer based on your contextual knowledge and what it says in **Interpretations A** and **B**.

EXAMINER TIP

There are 4 marks for Question 1 and 4 marks for Question 2. This means you should spend no more than 5 minutes answering each of them.

EXAMINER TIP

You have around 10 minutes to answer Question 3. Answering Questions 1 and 2 will help you become familiar with the interpretations, but do read them through again and look for points that you can support or challenge with your own knowledge.

RECAP

The Battle of the Little Big Horn (1876)

Events leading to the Battle of the Little Big Horn

Timeline

▼ 1868
- The Fort Laramie Treaty of 1868 says that no non-Indigenous person, apart from US government officials, 'shall ever be permitted to pass over, settle upon, or reside' in the Great Sioux Reservation, which included the sacred Paha Sapa (Black Hills).

▼ 1874
- In 1874, US Army Lieutenant Colonel George Custer leads an expedition into the Black Hills. The soldiers find gold and it starts a gold rush.

▼ 1875
- The US government tries to buy the Black Hills from the Lakota for $6 million. Chief Sitting Bull and other influential Lakota leaders refuse. The government then orders the Lakota and Cheyenne to return to their reservations by 31 January 1876 or be considered 'hostiles'. This is so the gold rush can go ahead without resistance from Indigenous bands.

▼ January 1876
- Several bands do not meet the deadline, including those led by Lakota chiefs Sitting Bull and Crazy Horse. They send messages to say they are hunting, because the reservations are short of supplies, and will return in the spring. The US government declares they are 'hostiles' and sends troops after them.

▼ March 1876
- US soldiers attack and destroy what they think is Sitting Bull's camp. It is actually a Cheyenne camp and this convinces the Cheyenne to join the fight.

▼ June 1876
- Lakota and Cheyenne forces, led by Crazy Horse, defeat US troops at the Battle of the Rosebud. The victorious bands travel to Sitting Bull's camp on Little Big Horn River.

Key events of the Battle of the Little Big Horn (25 June 1876)

① Scouts from the Seventh Cavalry found Sitting Bull's camp at Little Big Horn River. They advised caution because the camp was so large. General Custer ignored the advice and ordered an immediate attack.

② Major Reno led 110 cavalry soldiers in an attack. They were driven back by more than 500 warriors. Reno retreated quickly, leaving wounded men behind.

③ Custer attacked with 210 cavalry soldiers. Crazy Horse led an attack of 1,000 warriors against the soldiers.

④ All the US soldiers were killed within around half an hour of fighting. Cheyenne tradition says that a Cheyenne warrior called Buffalo Calf Road Woman knocked Custer off his horse.

⑤ The allies celebrated their victory in Sitting Bull's camp. Then, the next morning, the camp broke up as bands moved away. Many went back to their reservations.

The Lakota name for the Little Big Horn River is the Greasy Grass River, so they refer to the Battle of the Little Big Horn as the 'Battle of the Greasy Grass'.

APPLY

INTERPRETATION ANALYSIS

Read this interpretation.

▼ **INTERPRETATION A** *The last words of Crazy Horse, written down in 1877 by Jesse Lee, a US Army veteran who was working as an Indian agent when Crazy Horse surrendered in 1877. Here, Crazy Horse reflects on his long life and the reasons for conflict between Indigenous people and Euro-Americans:*

> My friend, I do not blame you for this. Had I listened to you this trouble would not have happened to me. I was not hostile to the white men. Sometimes my young men would attack the Indians who were our enemies and took their ponies. They did it in return. We had bison for food, and their hides for clothing and for our tipis. We preferred hunting to a life of idleness on the reservation, where we were driven against our will. At times we did not get enough to eat and we were not allowed to leave the reservation to hunt. We preferred our own way of living. We were no expense to the government when we lived that way. All we wanted was peace and to be left alone.

a Copy and complete this table by finding quotes from **Interpretation A** to support the statements in the first column.

Contextual understanding	Supporting quote from Interpretation A
1 Indigenous bands traditionally raided other nations for resources.	
2 The bison provided horse nations with everything they needed to live on the Plains.	
3 Indigenous people did not want to move to reservations.	
4 Reservation conditions were harsh, without enough to eat.	
5 Indigenous people recognised that reservations made them dependent on the US government.	

b How convincing do you find **Interpretation A** as an explanation for the reasons why the Lakota and Cheyenne fought the Battle of the Little Big Horn in June 1876?

DESCRIBE

a Look at this list of the problems the US government was causing the Lakota and Cheyenne by 1876. For each problem listed, add at least one piece of evidence.
- Treaties
- Gold
- Railroads
- Military campaigns
- Bison
- Reservations

b **EXAM QUESTION** Describe two problems facing the Lakota and Cheyenne by 1876.

REVIEW

Look back at pages 28 and 29 to remind yourself about the 'Indian Wars' and the Fort Laramie Treaty of 1868, as well as pages 44–47 to remind yourself about President Grant's Peace Policy and Euro-American attitudes to Indigenous people.

EXAMINER TIP

Focus on facts when answering 'describe' questions. These questions should not take you longer than 5 minutes to answer in an exam.

America 1840–1895 Expansion and Consolidation

 **RECAP**

Reactions to the Battle of the Little Big Horn

Euro-Americans were shocked that US cavalry soldiers could be defeated by 'savages'.

- Many demanded that the US government respond with a massive military campaign against 'hostile' Indigenous nations.
- However, some questioned whether the US Army's destructive tactics had caused the conflict.

▼ A c1900 drawing of the Battle of the Little Big Horn by Amos Bad Heart Bull, a member of the Lakota Nation, who was eight years old at the time of the battle

The US government's response

The US government used its military and industrial strength to destroy the power of the Lakota and Cheyenne Nations and their independence on the northern Plains.

A winter campaign in 1876–1877 was recommended by General Sheridan as a way of ensuring the nations would not be able to continue their resistance.

Timeline

▼ **July 1876**
- The US government sends reinforcements to the northern Plains and constructs two new forts.

▼ **August 1876**
- The US government cuts off all food rations to Lakota reservations until they agree to give up their rights to the Black Hills (Paha Sapa).
- US forces begin to attack Lakota and Cheyenne villages and camps, capturing supplies and horses.

▼ **Winter 1876**
- The US Army continues its campaign against the Lakota and Cheyenne. For example, in November 1876, during an attack on a Cheyenne camp, 173 lodges (homes) are burned, all the band's winter supplies are destroyed and 500 horses are captured and killed. This causes terrible suffering for survivors in the freezing winter conditions, forcing them to surrender or return to reservations.

▼ **February 1877**
- Congress passes an Act overturning the Fort Laramie Treaty of 1868. It takes the Black Hills (Paha Sapa) away from the Lakota and breaks up the rest of the Great Sioux Reservation into smaller reservations. The Act says the US government is now allowed to build roads across Lakota lands, breaks up the rest of the Great Sioux Reservation into smaller reservations, and opens up the remaining land for settlement.

▼ **May 1877**
- Crazy Horse and his band surrender to US forces.

▼ **May 1877**
- Sitting Bull and his band escape over the border to Canada.

▼ **September 1877**
- Crazy Horse is killed while resisting arrest, according to his US guards.

50 Chapter 8 Indigenous resistance

APPLY

INTERPRETATION ANALYSIS

Read this interpretation.

▼ **INTERPRETATION A** *Adapted from 'The Custer Battlefield', an article in the* Wyoming Tribune *newspaper, published in 1903. This article was written following a tour of the battlefield by the editor of the newspaper:*

> The Custer massacre of 1876 aroused the entire country. Troops were thrown into the northwest by the thousands, and the subjugation of the Sioux [Lakota] and other hostile tribes was soon accomplished.
>
> In the years that followed, the white man rose high above the defeat, building railroads and opening up the country. The proud victors of June 25, 1876, became the hopeless wards of the nation.

a How long after the Battle of the Little Big Horn was this interpretation written?

b 'Subjugation' is the act of bringing people under control and governing them in a way that allows them no freedom. Using your own knowledge, summarise the methods the US government used to subjugate the Lakota and the Cheyenne.

c Who is **Interpretation A** talking about when it mentions the 'victors of June 25, 1876'?

d What is meant by the term 'wards of the nation'?

e What opinion does **Interpretation A** give about the US government's response to the Battle of the Little Big Horn?

IN WHAT WAYS

a How did each of the following affect the Lakota?
  - The Fort Laramie Treaty of 1851
  - The Fort Laramie Treaty of 1868
  - The Act of 1877

b **EXAM QUESTION** In what ways were the lives of Indigenous peoples affected by government actions and laws?

REVIEW

Look back at page 26 to remind yourself about the Fort Laramie Treaty of 1851 and page 29 to remind yourself about the Fort Laramie Treaty of 1868.

 **RECAP**

The Dawes Act (1887)

The aims of the Dawes Act (1887)

By 1887, conditions on reservations were getting worse and worse. The USA blamed this on the way that Indigenous people shared resources and responsibilities.

The Dawes Act of 1887 wanted to break up Indigenous societies and force Indigenous people to assimilate into US society. It aimed to:

- encourage Indigenous people to become family farmers (like homesteaders)
- undermine the power of chiefs and Indigenous people's communal ways of living
- release more land for non-Indigenous settlers.

Features of the Dawes Act (1887)

1 Reservations divided into allotments
Reservation land was surveyed by government agents and broken up into allotments of 160 acres of farmland (or 320 acres of pasture for livestock).

2 Every individual given their own allotment
The allotments were divided among the Indigenous people on the reservation. Heads of households got 160 acres, people over 18 who weren't married and orphans under 18 got 80 acres, and children in a family got 40 acres each.

Features of the Dawes Act

5 US citizenship for some
Indigenous people who 'lived apart from their nation' and took on 'the habits of civilised life' could then become US citizens, with the right to vote (and pay taxes).

4 Restrictions for 25 years
An allotment couldn't be bought, sold or rented for 25 years because it was considered government property, but it could be passed on by inheritance.

3 Everything else opened for settlement
All the rest of the reservation land could then be sold to non-Indigenous settlers. The government kept the money received from the sale of this land to pay for the 'education and civilisation' of Indigenous people.

The consequences of the Dawes Act (1887)

- Nations had no legal power to stop the break-up of their reservations: the Dawes Act overruled all existing treaties. If individuals refused to select an allotment, one was chosen for them.
- Indigenous nations lost around 150 million acres under the Dawes Act.
- Once the 25-year period was up, many Indigenous people sold their land because they could not afford to start paying taxes on it.
- Non-Indigenous settlement increased, further breaking up Indigenous communities.

Indigenous residential schools

Indigenous residential schools were set up from the late 1870s, with the aim of assimilating young Indigenous people into US society.

- Between 1879 and 1918, over 10,000 Indigenous children were taken from reservations and sent to the Carlisle Indian Industrial School; just one of a number of residential schools established.
- Children and young people were forbidden from speaking their own languages or following their own spiritual beliefs. They had to dress in school uniform and were given new Americanised names. Boys had to cut off their long hair.

This attempt at assimilation didn't work. After leaving residential schools, some went on to fight for Indigenous rights within the US system, some returned to their reservations and felt they no longer belonged, and those who tried to integrate into US society faced constant racism.

APPLY

INTERPRETATION ANALYSIS

Read **Interpretation A** and **Interpretation B**.

▼ **INTERPRETATION A** *Adapted from a speech made by General George Crook in 1879. George Crook fought in the 'Indian Wars', the Civil War (for the Union) and in General Sherman's campaigns against Indigenous nations:*

> From my experience, the solution to the 'Indian problem' has always been obvious. Give these Indians little farms, survey them, let them put fences around them, let them have their own horses, cows, sheep, things that they can call their own, and it will do away with tribal Indians. Once an Indian sees that his food is secure, he does not care what the chief or any one else says.

▼ **INTERPRETATION B** *Adapted from a speech made by Chief Sitting Bull in 1877, retold to the author Charles Eastman. Charles Eastman was a Santee Dakota who attended college and medical school in the USA. He worked as a doctor on the Pine Ridge Reservation. He was told the words of Sitting Bull's speech by many men who were present:*

> We have now to deal with another race – small and feeble when our fathers first met them, but now great and overbearing. Strangely enough, they have a mind to till the soil, and the love of possessions is a disease with them. They claim this mother of ours, the Earth, for their own use, and fence their neighbors away from her, and deface her with their buildings and their refuse. They compel her to produce out of season, and when sterile she is made to take medicine in order to produce again. All this is sacrilege.

a Who is Sitting Bull talking about when he describes 'another race' who are now 'great and overbearing'? ('Overbearing' means unpleasantly proud of their own power.)

b What do you already know about Lakota beliefs about land? Does what you know fit with **Interpretation B**? Add notes around **Interpretation B**.

c What do you think **Interpretation A** means when it says 'do away with tribal Indians'? Use what you know about the aims of the Dawes Act of 1887 to help you answer this question.

d **EXAM QUESTION**

1 How does **Interpretation B** differ from **Interpretation A** about the relationship between Indigenous people and land? Explain your answer based on what it says in **Interpretations A** and **B**.

2 Why might the authors of **Interpretations A** and **B** have a different interpretation about the relationship between Indigenous people and land? Explain your answer using **Interpretations A** and **B** and your contextual knowledge.

3 Which interpretation gives the more convincing opinion about the relationship between Indigenous people and land? Explain your answer based on your contextual knowledge and what it says in **Interpretations A** and **B**.

REVIEW

Look back at page 14 to remind yourself about Lakota beliefs about land.

America 1840–1895 Expansion and Consolidation 53

 **RECAP**

Conditions on reservations

By the late 1880s, there were many challenges facing Indigenous nations because of US government attacks on their ways of life.

Nations were forced into being dependent on the government for food

- The deliberate extermination of bison herds forced nations to rely on government-issued food and clothing.
- Land used for hunting and gathering resources was lost as reservations were made smaller and allotments divided up reservation land.
- Reservations were often on the poorest land, and allotments were often hard to farm. Plus, farming on the Plains was challenging: droughts, fires and pests were common, and crops often failed.

Indigenous culture was deliberately suppressed

- Indigenous rituals and ceremonies, such as the Sun Dance ceremony, were banned.
- Many young Indigenous people were sent away to residential schools to be taught how to assimilate into Euro-American society.
- Indigenous people were moved away from sacred places that were essential to their identity, and pressured into replacing their beliefs with Christianity.

Nations were made less powerful and less independent

- Powerful nations were split up into a number of smaller reservations.
- After 1871, the US government treated Indigenous people as wards, not members of independent nations. There were no more treaties.
- The Dawes Act of 1887 divided communal lands into allotments and rewarded those who 'lived apart from their nation'. This undermined collective decision-making.
- After 1885, law enforcement on the reservations answered to the US government. This undermined the ability of nations to govern themselves.

The Wounded Knee Massacre (1890)

The Wounded Knee Massacre took place on 29 December 1890.

Timeline

▼ Summer 1890

- The Lakota do not have enough food: the bison have gone and a drought means crops do not grow.
- The US government decides to cut the usual food ration in half, to force Indigenous people to grow more of their own food.
- The Ghost Dance spreads across the Plains. Indigenous people recall all they have lost by dancing for a new world in which everything returns to how it had been before Euro-Americans arrived.

▼ 15 December 1890

- Having assumed the Ghost Dance is a war dance and that Indigenous people are preparing for an armed uprising, the US government bans it on all reservations.
- Following rumours that Sitting Bull is encouraging the Ghost Dance and planning a war against the USA, he is arrested at the Standing Rock Reservation.
- A crowd gathers, a shot is fired at the police and an Indigenous policeman fires his gun, killing Sitting Bull.

▼ 28 December 1890

- Some of Sitting Bull's band leave Standing Rock Reservation to join another chief, Spotted Elk. Spotted Elk decides to go to Pine Ridge Reservation to join up with Red Cloud and negotiate for peace.
- 500 soldiers led by Colonel James Forsyth, force Spotted Elk's group to surrender and camp at Wounded Knee Creek, guarded by soldiers with four cannons.

▼ 29 December 1890

- When the Lakota are ordered to give up all their weapons, there is fear and confusion.
- The US soldiers start shooting, and within ten minutes almost 300 Lakota have been massacred. More than half the dead are women and children.
- 25 US soldiers are killed, most of them shot by their own side by accident.

Responses to the Wounded Knee Massacre (1890)

- Some Euro-Americans said the 'Battle of Wounded Knee' was the Seventh Cavalry's revenge for the Battle of the Little Big Horn. They praised the US Army for preventing a Ghost Dance uprising.
- Many others did not agree. Colonel Forsyth was put on trial at a military court and newspaper commentators criticised the murder of innocent women and children.
- Indigenous people continued to dance the Ghost Dance in secret.

APPLY

INTERPRETATION ANALYSIS

Read this interpretation.

▼ **INTERPRETATION A** *Adapted from* General Miles's Indian Campaigns, *by George Baird, published in 1961. George Baird was an officer in the US Army, in the regiment commanded by General Miles. This interpretation was written after Baird retired in 1903:*

> The 'Messiah Craze' took shape from what was, unfortunately, an always-present feeling with the Indians – hunger. The Messiah was not only to annihilate the invading whites, but to bring back the boundless herds of bison which, only a decade ago, were the Indians' preferred food. The non-progressive, inveterately wild Indians, of whom Sitting Bull was the best known, saw an opportunity to recover their power. But due to the careful planning of General Miles, during the trouble, from November 15, 1890 to January 25, 1891, not a person was killed by Indians outside the boundaries of an Indian reservation, and the homes and property of nearby settlers were kept safe.

a The 'Messiah Craze' in **Interpretation A** is, as you'll have worked out already, the Ghost Dance. What does the interpretation say is the cause of the Ghost Dance?

b According to **Interpretation A**, what was the aim of the Ghost Dance?

c According to **Interpretation A**, what were the consequences of the Ghost Dance movement?

d How convincing do you find **Interpretation A** about the causes, aims and consequences of the Ghost Dance? What evidence would you use to back up your argument?

EXAMINER TIP

First, decide which reason was the more important one. To stretch yourself (to aim for top marks), can you also show how the reasons are connected to each other?

BULLET POINTS

a Draw a diagram to summarise the challenges facing Indigenous nations by the late 1880s. You could use colours and images to make your diagram memorable.

b Which of the following was the more important reason for the extermination of the bison:
- railroads
- government actions?

Explain your answer with reference to **both** bullet points.

REVIEW

Look back at pages 40–41 and 44–47 to remind yourself about the reasons for the extermination of the bison.

 **RECAP**

Theories about the frontier

The frontier was the imaginary line between areas settled by Euro-Americans and unsettled areas.

In 1890, the US census data showed that every area of the USA had people settled in it. As a result, the US census office concluded that there was no longer a frontier in the USA.

In response, a US historian called Frederick Jackson Turner wrote an influential essay in 1893. He defined the frontier as 'the meeting point between savagery and civilisation' and described how it had moved over time and had now disappeared altogether.

Indigenous peoples and the frontier

Turner's view of US history was very influential at the time. The idea that Indigenous peoples were destined to disappear as the frontier closed was powerful. The Wounded Knee Massacre was seen by many as the end of Indigenous peoples' role in American history.

Turner turned out to be wrong: Indigenous nations and Indigenous people did not disappear.

By resisting assimilation, Indigenous nations survived the expansion of the USA between 1840 and 1890, and in the years that followed. Today, Indigenous nations' identities and values are important and influential across North, Central and South America and globally.

SUMMARY

- President Grant's Peace Policy recognised problems with previous US government policies towards Indigenous nations.
- Grant's Peace Policy aimed to improve the administration of reservations, while at the same time increasing pressure on Indigenous people to assimilate into US society. These aims were 'humanitarian' aims, but Grant was happy for 'exterminator' methods to be used against 'hostiles'.
- Violent resistance continued, against the construction of the first transcontinental railroad and, after 1874, to miners prospecting for gold on sacred land in the Black Hills (Paha Sapa).
- The Battle of the Little Big Horn was a disaster for the US Army, but the US military campaign that followed it was a disaster for the Lakota and Cheyenne.
- The Dawes Act of 1887 attempted to force Indigenous people to become family farmers by splitting up reservation land into allotments, and selling the rest to settlers.
- The Ghost Dance was a form of cultural resistance, but the US government mistook it as the start of an armed uprising. Instead of an uprising, however, a massacre of 300 Lakota people took place in 1890 at Wounded Knee Creek.
- Although the US Census Office declared the frontier between settled and unsettled land closed in 1890, Indigenous resistance to the expansion of the USA continued.

70–89 Revision progress

APPLY

IN WHAT WAYS

a Look at the labels on the following map and make notes on how each of the following affected settlement in the West:
- the Indian Removal Act of 1830 and Indian Territory
- the Oregon Trail
- the Mormon migration to the Great Salt Lake Valley
- the California Gold Rush
- the Fort Laramie Treaty of 1851 and the Fort Laramie Treaty of 1868
- the completion of the first transcontinental railroad in 1869
- reservations.

▼ *An 1898 map showing the distribution of the population of the USA, created using data from the 1890 census*

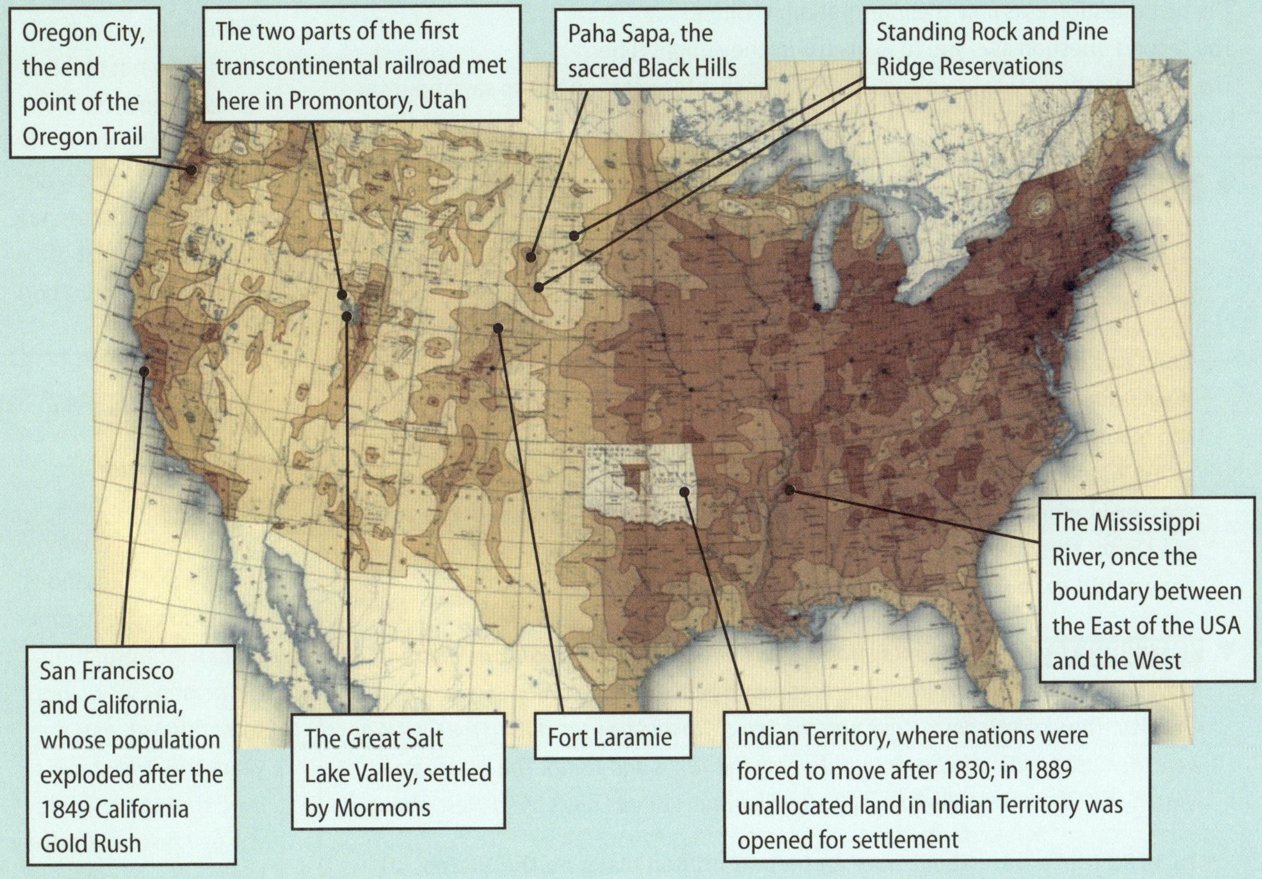

- Oregon City, the end point of the Oregon Trail
- The two parts of the first transcontinental railroad met here in Promontory, Utah
- Paha Sapa, the sacred Black Hills
- Standing Rock and Pine Ridge Reservations
- The Mississippi River, once the boundary between the East of the USA and the West
- San Francisco and California, whose population exploded after the 1849 California Gold Rush
- The Great Salt Lake Valley, settled by Mormons
- Fort Laramie
- Indian Territory, where nations were forced to move after 1830; in 1889 unallocated land in Indian Territory was opened for settlement

b **EXAM QUESTION** In what ways were the lives of people living in America affected by the expansion of the USA?

EXAMINER TIP

Exam questions are often structured to be as broad as possible, to give you the best chance to answer them using what you know. There are many possible answers to this question: you just need two or three relevant ways to write about, which ideally show that the expansion of the USA affected different groups in different ways.

REVIEW

Look back at page 16 for the Oregon Trail, pages 18 and 19 for Mormon settlement of the West, pages 20 and 21 for the California Gold Rush, page 24 for the Indian Removal Act of 1830, page 26 for the Fort Laramie Treaty of 1851 and page 29 for the Fort Laramie Treaty of 1868.

America 1840–1895 Expansion and Consolidation 57

Exam practice

GCSE sample answers

REVIEW

On these exam practice pages, you will find a sample student answer for each of the question types you will find in the America 1840–1895 section of your Paper 1 exam. What are the strengths and weaknesses of the answers? Read the following pages and think carefully about what the student has written, what the examiner has said about each answer, and how you might improve your own answers.

Interpretation analysis questions

Paper 1, Section A begins with three questions that ask you to work with two interpretations and their accompanying provenance (caption or label).

You will be asked three interpretations questions:

- The first question asks *how* the interpretations differ.
- The second question asks you to explain *why* they might differ.
- The third question asks you to *evaluate* what each interpretation has to say about the history involved.

▼ **INTERPRETATION A** Adapted from Black Elk Speaks, by John G. Neihardt, published in 1932. Black Elk (1863–1950) was a Lakota medicine man who fought at the Battle of the Little Big Horn. He was interviewed in 1932 by John Neihardt, who wrote down his words:

> They say that the last of the bison herd was slaughtered by the Wasichus [white people] in the autumn of 1883. I can remember when the bison were so many that they could not be counted, but more and more Wasichus came to kill them until there were only heaps of bones scattered where they used to be. The Wasichus did not kill the bison to eat them; they took only the hides to sell. They killed them for the gold they could earn – the metal that makes Wasichus crazy.

▼ **INTERPRETATION B** Adapted from a letter written by General William Sherman to William Cody in 1897. William Sherman was a general on the Union side during the Civil War. The violently destructive 'scorched earth' tactics he used during the Civil War were then used against Indigenous nations in the 1870s and 1880s. The letter was written to William Cody ('Buffalo Bill') after Sherman visited Cody's 'Wild West' show:

> In 1865 there were about nine and a half million bison on the Plains; all are now gone, killed for their meat, their skins, and their bones. This seems like desecration, cruelty, and murder, yet they have been replaced by twice as many cattle. At that date there were about 165,000 Pawnees, Sioux, Cheyennes, and Arapahoes, who depended upon these bison for their yearly food. They, too, have gone, but they have been replaced by twice or three times as many white men and women, who have made the earth blossom with their crops, and who can be counted, taxed, and governed by the laws of Nature and civilization.

EXAMINER TIP

While reading the interpretations, try to think about the key point each one makes and then how they are different from each other. Why not make notes around them or underline the things that are different? This is an excellent way to prepare to answer the first of the three interpretation questions.

EXAMINER TIP

It is really important to think about some possible reasons *why* the two interpretations might differ. Remember that an interpretation is a person's view about something at least five years after they have lived through it. There will be reasons why they hold that particular view, and this is what you need to identify in your answer to the second of the three interpretations questions. You should read the captions for the interpretations carefully because they will contain clues as to why each person thinks a certain way.

Revision progress

 1 How does **Interpretation B** differ from **Interpretation A** about bison hunting on the Plains?
Explain your answer based on what it says in **Interpretations A** and **B**.
4 marks

Now look at a student answer. Remember, this question is asking you to write about the ways in which the two interpretations are different.

Sample student answer
Interpretation A says that the way Euro-Americans killed all the bison was wasteful. The author says that Euro-Americans were greedy and that they 'did not kill them to eat' and 'took only the hides to sell', which means they took only the bison skins. It also says that bison disappeared because 'more and more Wasichus came to kill' the bison.

Interpretation B also says that the bison were all killed for their meat, their skins and their bones, but it says they have been replaced by 'twice as many cattle'.

OVERALL COMMENT
This would achieve a low Level 2. The student has provided a developed analysis of the content of Interpretation A but their analysis of Interpretation B is weaker. The answer needs to explain *how* the two interpretations are different.

 2 Why might the authors of **Interpretations A** and **B** have a different interpretation about bison hunting on the Plains?
Explain your answer using **Interpretations A** and **B** and your contextual knowledge.
4 marks

Look at the student answer. Remember, this question is asking you to write about *why* the interpretations are different. As a result, you will have to read the provenance very carefully.

Sample student answer
The author of Interpretation A was a Lakota medicine man so he probably would have had traditional Lakota views about how bison should be hunted.

The author of Interpretation B fought against Indigenous nations, which might have meant he thought that getting rid of the bison was the best way to control Indigenous people.

OVERALL COMMENT
This is a Level 1 answer. The student has identified two relevant reasons for the differences. To improve, they need to explain reasons for the differences. For example, they could have written about the beliefs that might have influenced each author. Lakota beliefs that all animals have spirits, and that disaster will follow if people do not respect these spirits, meant that wasting resources was viewed negatively. Euro-American belief in Manifest Destiny involved making the Plains useful and profitable, and justified clearing away obstacles, like the bison, that got in the way of 'progress'.

EXAMINER TIP
This question is very straightforward and is worth 4 marks.

EXAMINER TIP
The student broadly identifies the differences: that the writer of Interpretation A criticises the greedy and wasteful way the bison were hunted on the Plains by Euro-Americans, while the author of Interpretation B sees their destruction as worthwhile in the end because it meant the Plains could be 'civilised'.

EXAMINER TIP
It is vital that you look at who the author is, the time they were writing or speaking, their intentions and their intended audience. You will never really know why they said what they said, so you have to speculate. However, your answer can still be historically informed.

EXAMINER TIP
The student uses conditional words and phrases, such as 'probably' and 'might have'. Such a speculative approach is good when not all the facts are known.

Exam practice

> **EXAM QUESTION**
>
> **3** Which interpretation gives the more convincing opinion about bison hunting on the Plains?
>
> Explain your answer based on your contextual knowledge and what it says in **Interpretations A** and **B**.
>
> 8 marks

This question uses the key word 'convincing'. So, you need to focus on the history surrounding the issue mentioned in the question; in this case, bison hunting on the Plains.

In simple terms, you are being asked which interpretation is better, which one 'fits in' with what you have learned. One way to look at it is to think of the two interpretations as witnesses in a trial: which version, based on all you have learned in the topic, is most believable (or 'convincing')? Now look at the student answer.

Sample student answer

Interpretation A says that it was wrong for Euro-Americans to exterminate millions of bison in a wasteful way, and I find this opinion convincing.

The Indigenous nations of the Plains hunted bison too, but they were not wasteful: in fact, they used every part of the bison. For example, they made soap from bison fat and needles from bison bones. In contrast, once the first transcontinental railroad was completed in 1869, Euro-Americans were encouraged to visit the Plains to hunt as many bison as possible.

Interpretation B says this looked like 'desecration, cruelty, and murder', but that it was all worth it because there are now twice as many cattle on the Plains. Interpretation B also says that it was worth destroying the ways of life of Indigenous nations of the Plains so that Euro-Americans could settle there. However, we know that the farming practices used by Euro-American farmers led to terrible environmental problems by the 1930s. The earth did not 'blossom' with crops for very long.

For me it is convincing that killing all the bison was wasteful and I think it was a crime against Indigenous nations of the Plains.

> **EXAMINER TIP**
>
> Notice that there is no evidence to support the student's conclusion in the final paragraph. There should be. What evidence could the student have used to back up their point that the way the bison were hunted by Euro-Americans was a crime? You could think about the treaties signed by Indigenous nations.

OVERALL COMMENT

This answer reaches Level 3 because it contains detailed and specific knowledge about both interpretations.

OVER TO YOU

Read the sample answers again, but this time:

a In the first sample answer, highlight where it specifically mentions the *differences* between the two interpretations.

b In the second sample answer, highlight where it gives reasons *why* the two interpretations are different.

c In the third sample answer, highlight where it demonstrates factual knowledge.

d Finally, have a go at writing a series of answers yourself, making sure you closely follow the advice given here. You should spend about 5 minutes on Question 1, 5 minutes on Question 2, and 10 minutes on Question 3.

Revision progress

The 'describe' question

4 Describe two problems faced by Indigenous nations during the Civil War.

4 marks

Sample student answer

One problem was that the US government did not pay annuities when it should have done, because it was spending so much money fighting the southern states. Annuities were payments made to nations in return for giving up large areas of land and moving to a reservation. Because reservations were usually too small to feed everyone by hunting, and rarely contained good farming land, delays to annuity payments could mean starvation, which is what happened on the Lower Sioux Reservation in 1862 when the annuity payment did not arrive.

A second problem was that the US Army left the West to fight the southern states. Communities in the West then formed volunteer militias to protect themselves as they took more and more resources from Indigenous nations. These militias often had 'exterminator' views, which led to many attacks on Indigenous nations. For example, the Colorado militia attacked Black Kettle's band in what became known as the Sand Creek Massacre (1864) after Black Kettle had been told he would be safe at Sand Creek.

EXAMINER TIP

This paragraph clearly identifies one problem, and uses relevant facts and understanding to explain the problem. The student has not wasted time writing about things that are not identified in the question.

EXAMINER TIP

This paragraph clearly identifies a second problem, and also uses relevant facts and understanding to describe the problem. It is important that you identify (and describe) only *two* 'problems'. Don't waste time writing about three or four problems!

EXAMINER TIP

Other 'problems' you might identify could be the problems associated with the passing of the Homestead Act of 1862, which was only made possible because of the Civil War. The same applies to the construction of the first transcontinental railroad following the Pacific Railroad Act of 1862: in order to grant millions of acres of land to the railroad companies, new treaties were made that 'extinguished' Indigenous rights and pushed Indigenous people onto reservations.

OVERALL COMMENT

This is a top-level answer: it would achieve Level 2. The key to reaching the higher marks is not just to write down lots of factual information about the problem, the issue or the feature. You must also ensure that the answer explains why the aspect identified was a problem, and the student has done this in this answer.

OVER TO YOU

1. How would you improve the sample answer?
2. Now it's time for you to have a go at planning and writing an answer to this question. Spend no more than 5 minutes on your answer.
3. Now check your answer...
   - [ ] Did you name two problems?
   - [ ] For each problem, did you *expand* on it and *explore why* it was a problem for Indigenous nations?

If you are struggling to remember events affecting Indigenous nations in the Civil War years, reread pages 28–29 of this Revision Guide.

America 1840–1895 Expansion and Consolidation

Exam practice

The 'in what ways' question

 5 In what ways were people's lives affected by the Oregon Trail? Explain your answer. **8 marks**

Sample student answer

The Oregon Trail affected the lives of many thousands of migrants who travelled along it to reach Oregon and also California between around 1840 and 1869.

One effect that it had was good. It was a reliable way to get to the Far West overland, a 2,000 mile trip. Without the Oregon Trail, people would not have had a safe route for their wagons through the Rocky Mountains. By 1869, more than 400,000 people had migrated to the Far West along the Oregon Trail, and their lives changed completely. In the East, many did not have very good jobs and land was expensive. In Oregon, land was free and there was a chance they would find gold and become rich in California.

Another effect it had was not so positive: a lot of people died on the Oregon Trail. Diseases spread quickly through wagon trains. For example, cholera spread when migrants drank water from places where other migrants had gone to the toilet. Accidents were also really common. For example, migrants were sometimes crushed under wagon wheels. This means some people would have arrived in the Far West without loved ones who had died on the way, or who were disabled because of accidents that happened on the journey.

> **EXAMINER TIP**
> This is not an essay question. You must quickly write down the ways in which the Oregon Trail changed or affected the lives of different groups of people.

> **EXAMINER TIP**
> It is good that the student has mentioned conditions in the East. However, this is supporting information for a point that could be made more clearly. By contrasting the conditions that made people want to leave the East with the opportunities in the Far West, the answer could have done more to explain why the Oregon Trail transformed people's lives.

OVERALL COMMENT

The answer would achieve Level 3 for the detailed knowledge of the way the Oregon Trail affected the lives of one group of people: Euro-American migrants travelling to the Far West between around 1840 and 1869. Level 4 answers to these questions recognise that there were different effects on different groups of people who responded in different ways at different times. The Oregon Trail had significant effects on Indigenous people, and an answer contrasting the effects of the Oregon Trail on Euro-American migrants and Indigenous nations would be a good approach for a Level 4 answer to this question.

OVER TO YOU

1. How would you improve the sample answer?
2. Now it's time for you to have a go at planning and writing an answer to this question. Spend about 10 minutes on your answer.
3. Now check your answer. Did you do the following?
   - ☐ Did you name at least two ways in which the Oregon Trail affected people's lives?
   - ☐ For each way, did you add details to explain why it had an impact?

> **REVIEW**
> Go back to pages 16–17 of this Revision Guide to refresh your memory of the Oregon Trail.

Revision progress

The 'bullet points' question

6 Which of the following was the more important impact of the American Civil War on civilian populations:
- economic impacts
- social impacts?

Explain your answer with reference to **both** bullet points. **12 marks**

Sample student answer

The economic impacts of the Civil War were huge. After the war, US industrialisation really took off and there was very rapid economic growth in the North. This was important for civilians because it created lots of jobs, and also attracted millions of immigrants from Europe who boosted the economic growth even more.

The economic impacts of the Civil War were really important for civilians in the South too, but not in a good way. Cotton remained the South's main export, but after the war cotton prices fell because other countries started selling cotton. As a result, the 11 ex-Confederate states remained the poorest part of the USA for the next 100 years. Incomes fell by 40 per cent in the South after the war, for those civilians who had been paid wages before the war.

In the South, slavery was abolished by the Thirteenth Amendment (1865). Cotton farming was profitable because of the unpaid work of enslaved Black Americans, so this social change undermined the economy in the South. Many white southerners also refused to accept this social change. They responded by developing the Black Codes, laws that aimed to control freedpeople and keep them dependent on their employers, in a similar way to slavery.

In conclusion, I think the social impacts were more important.

EXAMINER TIP

The aim of the 'bullet points' question is to get you to show that you know about the reasons, events and consequences of the period in American history you have studied. You might be asked to focus on results, impacts or causes. You also have to reach a judgement (conclusion) that relates to the question.

EXAMINER TIP

The answer goes into detail about the economic impacts in both the North and the South.

OVERALL COMMENT

This answer would achieve a Level 3. This conclusion is weak. The question asks which had the *more important* impact. The student states that the social impacts were greater than the economic ones, but needs to explain their reasons for reaching this conclusion.

OVER TO YOU

1 Have a go at writing a conclusion that would enable this answer to reach a Level 4.

Now check your answer. Did you do the following?

☐ state which impact was more important?

☐ explain your reason or reasons for this judgement?

☐ make sure the reason or reasons were the ones you had already discussed in your answer?

You may want to review pages 34–35 to refresh your knowledge of the economic and social impacts of the Civil War.

America 1840–1895 Expansion and Consolidation

Activity answers guidance

The answers provided here are examples, based on the information provided in the Recap sections of this Revision Guide. There may be other factors that are relevant to each question, and you should draw on as much of your own knowledge as possible to give detailed and precise answers. There are also many ways of answering exam questions (for example, of structuring an essay). However, these exemplar answers should provide a good starting point.

Chapter 1 Page 13

DESCRIBE

a Table could include the following points:

Dry climate: Challenge: there wasn't enough water to grow enough food. Dealt with: getting the resources they needed from hunting bison, from raiding other nations, and from trade.

Few trees: Challenge: there was very little wood for building, tools or fuel. Dealt with: using bison products in place of timber for all but a few essentials.

Cold winters: Challenge: hard to keep warm in cold weather without wood for buildings and fuel. Dealt with: dressing warmly in robes made from furry bison hides, and burning dried bison dung for fuel inside well-designed tipis.

Fast-moving animals: Challenge: they were hard to hunt on foot. Dealt with: using horses to hunt these animals, especially bison.

Scattered resources: Challenge: not enough resources in one place to support a community. Dealt with: being nomadic, travelling from place to place to find the resources needed.

b Like a desert, the Plains were too dry for Euro-American farming methods. Also, this name involves rejecting Indigenous ways of living on the Plains as not acceptable to Euro-Americans.

c Answer should describe two problems in detail. For example: the climate (using the information from the table to discuss the dry climate, cold winters and lack of trees) and scattered resources (using the information from the table to discuss the scattered resources and fast-moving animals).

Page 15

INTERPRETATION ANALYSIS

a Who owned Oregon Territory: Britain or the USA.

b By settling Oregon Territory with US citizens.

c As a pioneer, he is likely to have a positive view of people who travelled to new areas of the USA to settle.

d Manifest Destiny is the belief that God had given the USA a mission to expand its territory, culture and values to all of America, and the author says he predicted 'a great American community would grow up' on the west coast of the continent, and sees it as right that the USA should own Oregon completely if US citizens settled there in enough numbers.

Chapter 2 page 17

DESCRIBE

a Table could include the following points:

'Free land' in the Far West: Description: In the 1840s, Euro-American migrants could claim a square mile of land in the Far West for free. Pull or push factor? Pull.

Farming conditions in the Far West: Description: California and Oregon had a good climate for farming, and fertile soil. Pull or push factor? Pull.

Stories from migrants who had made the trip west: Description: People who had made the journey west encouraged others to join them. Pull or push? Pull.

Discovery of gold in the Far West: Description: In 1848, gold was discovered in California and people rushed there to get rich. Pull or push? Pull.

Economic depression in the East: Description: There was an economic depression in the East in the 1840s and people found it hard to make a living, especially farmers in states like Ohio. Pull or push? Push.

Expensive land in the East: Description: Land was expensive in the East, making it hard to grow enough crops to make money. Pull or push? Push.

b The Oregon Trail made it possible for more people to migrate west overland because it was the first reliable route through the Rocky Mountains.

c Answer should describe two problems in detail. For example:

- An economic depression in the East in the 1840s meant people found it hard to make a living. In contrast, California and Oregon had a good climate and fertile soil for farming, which encouraged people to go west to make a better life for themselves and their families.
- Land was expensive in the East, making it hard to grow enough crops to make money. In the Far West, migrants could claim a square mile of land for free, which was very tempting for many.

Page 19

INTERPRETATION ANALYSIS

Answers might include:

a Convincing. Mormons did find ways to tackle the challenges presented by Utah's environment. For example, they copied Indigenous techniques, such as making dams in creeks to store fresh water and using adobe to build houses, and they carefully planned settlements so they grew enough food for their inhabitants.

b Convincing. By 1870, over 70,000 Mormons had migrated to the Great Salt Lake Valley, supported by the Perpetual Emigration Fund and the carefully organised Mormon Trail.

c Convincing. Each family was given half an acre of land on which to build a home and plant crops, and each settlement also had a square mile of fields for crops, so people had a place to live, food to eat and support from the rest of the community.

d Unconvincing. Mormons settled on Indigenous land in the Great Salt Lake Valley and learned how to live in Utah's challenging environment from Indigenous people. Indigenous people had been living in the area for thousands of years and were unlikely to need help from the newly arrived Mormons.

BULLET POINTS

a Free land in the Far West; good climate for farming and fertile soil in the Far West; gold discovered in California; economic depression in the East; land expensive in the East.

b A good answer will explain that religious reasons were important because the main reason 70,000 Mormons had migrated to the Great Salt Lake Valley by 1870 was the desire to live under Mormon laws and leadership, and escape religious persecution in the East. Many non-Mormons said Mormon beliefs were blasphemous, and the Mormon leader Joseph Smith was murdered by a mob.

A good answer will then consider the economic reasons for the Mormon migration: many Mormons living in the East were poor and couldn't afford the trip, so the Perpetual Emigration Fund was set up in 1849 to help Mormons migrate to the Great Salt Lake Valley. Without the fund, it is doubtful migration to the area would have increased as much as it did in the 1840s.

A good answer will go on to consider the economic reasons non-Mormons migrated west, comparing the number of Mormons who migrated west (70,000 by 1870) with the number of non-Mormons who migrated west (400,000 along the Oregon Trail by 1869). The answer could also acknowledge that religious beliefs – such as the belief in Manifest Destiny – may have been important for these migrants as well.

A good answer will end with a conclusion that states and justifies that economic reasons were more important.

Page 21

IN WHAT WAYS

a Table could include the following points:

Indigenous people: Impacts: In order to mine for gold, Euro-Americans stole land by defrauding, tricking or forcing Indigenous nations off their land. Indigenous people were killed, their environment was degraded and poisoned, and their rights were disregarded.

Chinese miners: Impacts: Euro-Americans forced Chinese miners away from new claims. They were violently attacked and law officers did nothing to protect them. As a result, many went to work building the new railroads.

Euro-Americans: Impacts: Very few became rich finding gold, but Euro-American business owners made lots of money and many started farming or found jobs working as farm labourers. Men and women will have had very different experiences.

b A good answer will use the information from the table to consider the different ways the California Gold Rush affected the lives of different groups of people living in the USA.

64 Activity answers guidance

The discussion will be supported by detailed information about each group.

Page 23

BULLET POINTS

a Answers might make the following points:

1841: The Nauvoo Legion is formed. The US government was unhappy because it did not like the way Mormons wanted to govern themselves, including having their own military force.

1856: US politicians criticise polygamy among Mormons. Polygamy is marrying more than one person at a time.

1857: President Buchanan sends soldiers to Utah Territory. The soldiers are sent because the US government had decided to replace Brigham Young with a non-Mormon governor and soldiers were needed to make sure US laws were being obeyed.

1857: The Mountain Meadow Massacre takes place. It occurs because the Mormons were expecting to be attacked by the US Army and Brigham Young had declared martial law.

b A good answer will explain that differences in ways of life were an important reason. The Mormons wanted to live independently and follow their own laws and practices, including polygamy, but the US government would not allow this. Mormons had faced discrimination and religious persecution in the East, including the murder of their leader Joseph Smith, and it is likely they feared the US Army was being sent to persecute them again when 25,000 soldiers were sent to Utah Territory to make sure US laws were being obeyed.

A good answer will then consider the actions of the US government as an important reason. It seems very unlikely that the Mountain Meadow Massacre and the Utah War would have happened in the way they did if President Buchanan had not decided to send 25,000 soldiers to Utah Territory. It was guaranteed to make the Mormons think they were going to be attacked, and was certainly the reason why Brigham Young declared martial law in August 1857 and why the Mormon leadership encouraged local Indigenous people to raid migrant wagon trains.

A good answer will end with a conclusion that states and justifies which reason was more important. There is no right or wrong answer, but the choice needs to be justified. For example, you could argue that the actions of the US government were the more important reason because the US government refused to accept the Mormons' wish to govern themselves but at the same time did not do enough to protect Mormons from discrimination and persecution. Or you could argue that, because Mormons refused to obey US laws as a result of their religious beliefs, it was inevitable that conflict would occur with the US government as soon as the Mormons living in the Great Salt Lake Valley were once again part of the USA.

Chapter 3 Page 25

IN WHAT WAYS

a Indian agents were US government officials who supervised the reservations and controlled the supplies that reached Indigenous people. They affected the lives of Indigenous people living on reservations because they could decide, for example, not to pay annuities, or to hold them back, if reservation rules were broken.

Annuities were a fixed amount of money paid to Indigenous nations every year in return for giving up large areas of land and moving to reservations. They were sometimes paid in goods of the same value. They affected the lives of Indigenous peoples living on reservations because they made Indigenous people dependent on the US government for things they used to provide for themselves.

b Table could include the following points:

Food: Living independently: Hunted bison on horseback, using every part of the bison, which was their main source of food, clothing and shelter.

Leadership: Living on reservations: Indian agents supervised reservations and controlled the supplies that reached Indigenous people; they had all the power, not the chiefs.

c A good answer will use the information in the first column of the table to consider the ways in which the lives of Indigenous people belonging to nations that moved to reservations changed. It will then go on to use the second column of the table to discuss how the lives of Indigenous people belonging to nations that remained independent and free in the 1850s, such as the Lakota, changed very little. The discussion will be supported by detailed information about each group.

Chapter 4 Page 27

INTERPRETATION ANALYSIS

a The interpretation accurately describes one of the US government's aims: concentrating Indigenous nations in their own separate territories, away from the overland trails. It also accurately describes that one of the terms of the treaty was that Euro-American migrants were not permitted to enter the lands set aside for the Indigenous nations that signed the treaty, and that the US government would act if any one of the eight nations experienced 'depredations' by US citizens. However, it is not accurate when it states that the treaty 'gave' the Indigenous nations 'the country which they now have'. The land in question was already Indigenous land, and the treaty simply established the boundaries of each nation's territory for the US government. The interpretation also leaves out other US government aims for the treaty, including reducing conflict between Indigenous nations, allowing the US government to build roads through Indigenous territory and paying an annuity of $50,000 to the nations each year.

b The interpretation gives a positive account of the treaty, stating that when 'some of our young people' wanted to search for gold in areas forbidden to Euro-Americans by the treaty, the US government stopped this from happening. But this is not an accurate description of how generally *unsuccessful* the Fort Laramie Treaty of 1851 was. For example, the failure of the treaty to prevent Euro-American migrants from crossing Indigenous land to prospect for gold in Montana was a key reason for Red Cloud's War (1866–1868).

BULLET POINTS

a Yes, the Permanent Indian Frontier did aim to keep Indigenous nations and US citizens away from each other. No, the Permanent Indian Frontier did not involve annuities.

b A good answer will explain that changes in US government policy were important because the Fort Laramie Treaty of 1851 involved a rejection of the policy of the Permanent Indian Frontier and focused on concentrating Indigenous nations in their own separate territories, away from the overland trails. However, both the Permanent Indian Frontier and the Fort Laramie Treaty of 1851 aimed to keep Indigenous nations and US citizens away from each other, so it can be argued the changes in US government policy were not significant enough to be the more important reason.

A good answer will then consider changes in reasons for migration west as an important reason. The California Gold Rush and the growth in California's economy that followed led to the huge increase in migration over the Permanent Indian Frontier and through Indigenous nations' territories from 1848 onwards. Without the prospect of becoming rich, few of these migrants would have made the long and difficult journey to the Far West, and it was the tensions caused by the huge increase in migrants travelling across the Plains that led to the Fort Laramie Treaty of 1851. However, it was not inevitable that the US government would abandon the Permanent Indian Frontier (it could have decided to honour the policy and prevent migrants crossing into Indigenous territory), so it can be argued that changes in reasons for migration west were not the most important reason.

A good answer will end with a conclusion that states and justifies which reason was more important. There is no right or wrong answer, but the choice needs to be justified.

Page 29

BULLET POINTS

a
- US Army forts in the West were left more or less defenceless, making it easier for Indigenous nations to attack them without opposition.
- Members of the militias often had 'exterminator' views and the militias launched murderous attacks on Indigenous bands.
- Migrants wanted fast routes to the goldfields, which meant they trespassed on Indigenous land, leading to retaliation by Indigenous bands. The Fort Laramie Treaty of 1851 prohibited this trespassing,

but the US government did not act. Meanwhile, migrants were demanding protection from Indigenous attacks.

b A good answer will explain that the Civil War was an important reason because it meant the US government's control over the West was weakened. The US Army left the West to fight the southern states. This meant there was more opportunity for Indigenous nations to resist colonisation without this resistance being met with opposition from the US Army. Settlers then formed local militias, some of which launched murderous attacks on Indigenous bands, such as the Sand Creek Massacre of 1864. More and more Indigenous bands then became convinced that they should join the 'Indian Wars'.

A good answer will then consider that the gold rushes were an important reason. When gold was found in Colorado in 1858, 100,000 migrants travelled through Cheyenne and Arapaho lands to reach Pike's Peak. The Fort Laramie Treaty of 1851 prohibited this, but the US government did not act. Later, Red Cloud's War (1866–1868) occurred because thousands of migrants followed the Bozeman Trail to the goldfields of Montana, across Lakota hunting grounds, against the Fort Laramie Treaty of 1851.

One conclusion might be that Red Cloud's War occurred after the Civil War (1861–1865), making gold rushes a more important reason. However, as with all 'bullet point' questions, there isn't one correct answer. A good answer will end with a conclusion that states and justifies which reason was more important.

Chapter 5 Page 31
INTERPRETATION ANALYSIS

a Table could include the following points:

Who is the author? A: Stephen F. Hale, a secession commissioner. B: Jefferson Davis, president of the Confederate States of America during the Civil War.

When was each written? A: 1860, just before the Civil War started in 1861. B: 1881, 16 years after the Civil War ended in 1865.

Why was it written? A: to make links between Alabama and Kentucky about plans to leave the Union. B: to justify the reasons for secession and Davis's actions during the war.

What was the main tension that led to the Civil War? A: The North's 'unrelenting and fanatical war' on the South over slavery. B: Not slavery but the 'persistent struggle' of the North to make itself more powerful than the South by excluding the South from benefitting from the expansion of the USA.

b 1 Interpretation B states that the main tension that led to the Civil War was not slavery but the 'persistent struggle' of the North to make itself more powerful than the South by excluding the South from benefitting from the expansion of the USA. In contrast, Interpretation A says the main tension was the North's 'unrelenting and fanatical war' on the South over slavery.

2 One reason for difference could be to do with when the interpretations were written: Interpretation A was written before the Civil War when southern states were planning to leave the Union but did not know that war would follow, and Interpretation B was written after the war when the Confederacy had been defeated. Another reason for difference could be to do with why the authors were writing: Interpretation A was written to persuade Kentucky to join Alabama in leaving the Union so focused on a common cause, while Interpretation B was written to justify Jefferson's reasons for fighting the Civil War (he didn't want to be seen as fighting against freedom, but instead as a defender of Confederate states' position within the Union). A good answer only needs to discuss one reason.

3 Interpretation A contains a lot of information that you know to be true about the South, which could make it more convincing. The economy of the South was heavily dependent on the labour of enslaved people to grow cotton. There was a lot of support for abolition in the North. Even though Lincoln said he would not get rid of slavery in states where it already existed, many in the South believed he planned to abolish it throughout the USA; and they were proved right in 1863 when Lincoln declared Emancipation.

Interpretation B could also be convincing because the expansion of the USA was a major reason for tensions between North and South, especially in Kansas. Kansas was created in 1854 by the Kansas–Nebraska Act, when it looked likely that Nebraska would become a free state, so that Kansas could potentially become a slave state. However, opposition to slavery in Kansas increased as thousands moved there from the North, and abolitionist John Brown attacked pro-slavery settlers, increasing tensions.

You will know that slavery was a long-term cause of tension between North and South, and the most significant cause of secession and therefore the Civil War, so your answer might conclude that Interpretation A is more convincing as a result.

Page 33
IN WHAT WAYS

a • Both sides introduced conscription during the Civil War and it caused problems because not all civilians wanted to fight. In the North, there were riots against conscription, and thousands travelled to Canada to escape conscription.
- Shortages and inflation caused problems to civilians during the Civil War because it meant it wasn't possible to buy everything that people needed and prices were too high for things to be affordable even if they were available. The situation was worse in the South than in the North.

b Table could include the following points:

Black Americans in the South: Economic impacts: Most Black Americans remained enslaved during the Civil War; some land was given to freed Black families. Social impacts: In 1863, President Lincoln declared the Emancipation of all enslaved people in Confederate states. Enslaved people knew that if they could reach Union forces in the South they would be free.

Black Americans in the North: Economic impacts: There were many more jobs for Black people in northern cities. Social impacts: Black Americans experienced prejudice and discrimination from white Americans who accused them of taking 'their' jobs.

White Americans in the South: Economic impacts: Shortages and inflation were very bad in the South because the North blockaded southern ports. Social impacts: Conscription meant women, older people and children had to take on men's roles in farming.

White Americans in the North: Economic impacts: Shortages and inflation were an issue but less problematic than in the South. Social impacts: there were riots against conscription, and thousands travelled to Canada to escape conscription; there were concerns about increasing numbers of Black Americans coming to work in northern cities.

c A good answer will use the information from the table to consider the different ways the lives of civilians were affected by the Civil War. The discussion will be supported by detailed information about each group.

Chapter 6 Page 35
INTERPRETATION ANALYSIS

a The Union

b He may have come to understand Black people better than most white Americans after working closely with them in conflict situations.

c He believes that Black Americans deserved all the rights of US citizens.

Page 37
INTERPRETATION ANALYSIS

a For example: Emma Falconer says that freedpeople assumed the Freedmen's Bureau would feed them and clothe them so they did not have to work and that, when the Freedmen's Bureau could not do this, Black people turned to stealing and arson.

b For example: The US government recognised that freedpeople were starting their new lives with nothing, so the Freedmen's Bureau did provide help with food and clothing. However, it also provided legal advice about work contracts. And, when asked, freedpeople said they most wanted help with education.

c She blames them for taking charge and using their powers to put Black Americans (who had opposed the Confederacy) rather than white supporters of the Confederacy in positions of power.

d For example: It is likely that the Ku Klux Klan (KKK) aimed to protect white communities from the threat to their ways of life caused by Reconstruction. However, by not condemning the KKK's actions, her interpretation implies that the KKK was a good thing. White supremacist organisations, formed to stop Black people voting by using violence and intimidation, are never a good thing!

BULLET POINTS

a For example:
- Radical Republican: the Black Codes show that many people in the Southern states want to keep freedpeople dependent on their employers in a similar way to slavery. The Black Codes show that a future Congress might repeal the Civil Rights Act of 1866 so, to ensure all US citizens have the same rights, the Fourteenth Amendment needs to be made part of the US Constitution.
- President Johnson: federal government should interfere as little as possible in the right of states to govern themselves. We must leave it to states to decide what is right for their people.

b A good answer will explain that the Black Codes were an important reason for the Fourteenth Amendment because it became clear that the southern states were not going to accept the Thirteenth Amendment and were systematically undermining the rights of Black Americans whenever they could. The Black Codes showed that many people in the southern states wanted to keep freedpeople dependent on their employers in a similar way to slavery. They also showed that a future Congress might repeal the Civil Rights Act of 1866 so, to ensure all US citizens had the same rights, the Fourteenth Amendment needed to be made part of the US Constitution.

A good answer will then consider that the Radical Republicans were an important reason. President Johnson believed federal government should interfere as little as possible in the right of states to govern themselves. He opposed the Reconstruction Act, which put each ex-Confederate state under military control until it had voted in a new constitution and approved the Thirteenth and Fourteenth Amendments. It was the Radical Republicans, who dominated Congress, who pushed the Act through.

A good answer will end with a conclusion that states and justifies which reason was more important. One possible conclusion is that, regardless of President Johnson's views or the actions of the Radical Republicans, if the southern states had accepted the Thirteenth Amendment and the Civil Rights Act of 1866 there would have been no reason for the Fourteenth Amendment, supporting the argument that the Black Codes were the main reason.

Chapter 7 Page 39
INTERPRETATION ANALYSIS

a For example: Many homestead farmers got into debt to buy farming equipment, but then never made enough from their farms to pay what they owed on time. Other homestead farmers discovered the farming equipment they had bought needed to be replaced before the loans were paid off.

b Because, although they could get land cheaply, most did not have the money to buy the equipment they needed to farm the land successfully.

c When homestead farmers were unable to repay the loans they had taken out, lenders recovered at least some of the money they were owed by seizing possessions, including land, selling them and keeping the money. The homestead farmers were then unable to 'prove up' their homesteads.

DESCRIBE

a
- Homesteads were small family farms established on land granted by the US government, whereas plantations were enormous farms farmed by workers. Enslaved people were forced to do the work on plantations until the end of the Civil War.
- Southern states blocked attempts to make land affordable because they knew more homesteaders would mean more free states (as homesteader farms wouldn't be able to sell crops as cheaply as the plantations that used enslaved labour). An increase in free states would weaken the South in Congress.
- They wanted the security of legal title to their land. Without legal title, their land could be taken away from them.
- Because, once the southern states had left the Union, their representatives were no longer in Congress to block a Homestead Act as they had always done before.

b One reason why the US government could consider it a success is the large number of claims: 4 million in total. One from the following reasons why the Homestead Act could be considered a failure: the high rate of failure (60 per cent of homesteaders didn't 'prove up'); rich people weren't prevented from making lots of claims and selling them on for profit; 160 acres was too small and the original act had to be extended with the Timber Culture Act of 1873. The answer should include a judgement about whether the Homestead Act was a success or a failure.

c Answer should describe two problems in detail. For example: problems passing the Homestead Act (using the information from part a to discuss opposition to the act from southern states) and the Homestead Act itself (using the information from part b to discuss the reasons why the act was a failure). Answer could also look ahead and consider the problems associated with farming the Plains.

Page 41
INTERPRETATION ANALYSIS

a The clause in the act that granted the railroad companies alternate sections of land along the railroad line was used to take land from Indigenous reservations and open it up to non-Indigenous settlement.

b You should recognise the policy of giving the two transcontinental railroad companies 10 square miles of land for every mile of track they built.

c You should know that the Cherokees were one of the nations forced to leave their homelands in the East following the Indian Removal Act of 1830. The area they settled in was provided by treaties in what became known as Indian Territory. This fits with the guarantees 'given in return for their homes east of the Mississippi' mentioned in Interpretation A.

d Reasons to find it convincing include the fact that it fits with what you know about the alternate sections of land granted to the railroad companies by the Pacific Railroad Act of 1862 and what you know about the Indian Removal Act of 1830. The treatment of Indigenous people it describes also fits with what you know about the US government's terrible record of protecting the rights of Indigenous nations despite signing treaties promising to protect those rights.

e The reasons why Interpretation A is convincing are discussed in part d above.

Interpretation B could also be considered convincing because we know that the two railroad companies made a lot of money. They were loaned enormous sums by the US government ($16,000 for every mile of track they built, and $48,000 per mile in the mountains), and sold 200 million acres of the land they were given by 1880.

However, Interpretation B becomes less convincing when it talks about the impact of the railroads on Indigenous people. It says that the railroads 'did more than anything else to … curb hostile Indians', but we know that nations resisted the railroads. As Interpretation A says, the railroads were 'dangerous to their interests and their peace in the future'.

Alternatively, you could argue that Interpretation B is more convincing because, by bringing settlers and bison hunters to the Plains, the transcontinental railroad forced Indigenous people to give up their traditional ways of life and move onto reservations.

Page 43
BULLET POINTS

a
- John Deere's steel plough could break up the sod (the thick layer of soil and grass held together with tangled roots) that covered the Plains. Previously, the sod broke cast iron ploughs and farmers had to dig fields by hand (which was exhausting) or hire professional 'sod-busters' (which was expensive).
- Joseph Glidden's barbed wire was used for fencing and it made protecting crops from cattle or wild animals much easier. Previously, homesteaders were importing very expensive wood because the Plains were too dry for trees to grow.

b Farmers on the Plains could send crops to markets in the East and the Far West by rail, and order new machinery from the East to tackle the problems of farming the Plains.

c   Answers might include:

A good answer will explain that transcontinental railroads were important because they brought farmers to the Plains safely. It was no longer necessary for them to make long and dangerous trips by wagon. The railroad companies ran huge campaigns to persuade people to buy their land, including marketing campaigns in European countries. By 1880, the railroad companies had sold 200 million acres in the West for settlement, and much of it was bought by farmers. This laid the foundations for successful farming on the Plains. Farmers on the Plains could also send crops to markets in the East and the Far West by rail, and order new machinery from the East to tackle the problems of farming the Plains.

A good answer will then consider how agricultural inventions were important. They solved some of the problems of farming the Plains and, if these problems had not been solved, farming on the Plains would not have been so successful. For example, John Deere's steel plough could break up the sod (the thick layer of soil and grass held together with tangled roots) that covered the Plains. Previously, the sod broke cast iron ploughs and farmers had to dig fields by hand (which was exhausting) or hire professional 'sod-busters' (which was expensive). Joseph Glidden's barbed wire was used for fencing and it made protecting crops from cattle or wild animals much easier. Previously, homesteaders were importing very expensive wood because the Plains were too dry for trees to grow.

A good answer will end with a conclusion that states and justifies which reason was more important. There is no right or wrong answer, but the choice needs to be justified. You could conclude that railroads were more important because, without railroads, the new agricultural inventions would not have been transported to the Plains cheaply enough for farmers to afford them. The railroads also brought the farmers to the Plains. However, you could also conclude that without ways to solve the problems of farming the Plains, fewer people would have been able to make a success of farming the Plains.

Chapter 8 Page 45
INTERPRETATION ANALYSIS

a   He convinced a large number of Indigenous people to move to the reservation; he persuaded more Indigenous people to start farming.

b   President Grant's Peace Policy wanted Indigenous people to stop hunting and start farming: this fits with the Indian agent's actions. In order to persuade Indigenous people to move to the reservation and start farming, the Indian agent must have gained their respect: this fits with the Peace Policy's aim of improving the quality of Indian agents.

c   The author is positive about E.P. Smith: 'by his policy of dealing with and encouraging them, [he] persuaded more Indians to start farming than all the agents here have since succeeded in doing'.

DESCRIBE

a   • Christian Churches should run reservations and missionaries should act as Indian agents.
    • US Army forts would stop settlers taking any more reservation land.
    • Reservations must be supplied properly, so people did not become desperate from hunger and/or Indigenous people on reservations must be forced to start farming to feed themselves.
    • No new treaties would be made. It became the federal government's responsibility to make sure Indigenous people assimilated into US society.

b   Answer should describe two problems in detail. For example: Reservations were often run by corrupt Indian agents who held back annuities and food rations. When, or if, food supplies did arrive, they were sometimes terrible quality. Some agents used starvation as a way of controlling Indigenous people. This increased tension between Indigenous people and the US government, and President Grant wanted peace, not conflict.

Page 47
INTERPRETATION ANALYSIS

a   Treating Indigenous people as enemies makes them more hostile towards the USA, while treating them as friends reduces them to poverty.

b   He says the Canadian system is 'permanent, decided, and just', which means it doesn't change, is clear and definite, and is fair. He also says that there has been less immigration to Canada than there has been to the USA, so the Canadians have been able to allow Indigenous people to live as they want rather than forcing them to assimilate.

c   You might conclude that Nelson Miles was best placed to understand the 'Indian problem' because of his leading role in military campaigns against Indigenous people, and because Isabella Bird was a British explorer who had not spent that much time in the USA. However, it's also possible to argue that Isabella Bird, as a visitor to the USA, would have had a clearer and more objective view of what she observed, when compared to someone who fought against Indigenous people and, perhaps, lost friends and colleagues in battle.

d 1 Interpretation B compares the USA to Canada and concludes that the Canadian system of 'managing' Indigenous nations is better than the USA's system. In contrast, Interpretation A identifies specific problems with the reservation system in the USA.

  2 Interpretation B was written by someone with a lot of experience of fighting Indigenous nations on the Plains. His relationships with Indigenous people were, therefore, primarily with people in conflict with the USA. In contrast, Interpretation A was written by someone from outside the USA, whose experience of Indigenous people might have been more objective and less biased, although it could also have been based on what non-Indigenous people told her about Indigenous people.

  3 Interpretation A is convincing because it mentions both 'exterminator' and 'humanitarian' attitudes, which means it covers both Euro-American perspectives of the 'Indian problem'. It also convincingly explains how both attitudes contributed towards the creation of the 'problem': treating Indigenous people as enemies makes them hostile, taking away their means to support themselves makes them dependent. What Interpretation A says about poverty on the reservations and fraud and corruption in the Indian Agency fits with what we know happened on reservations. We also know that gold rushes led to Indigenous people being forced off their land.

  Interpretation B is also convincing. While we may not know about Canada in this period, the point about US policy not being permanent rings true because it did change. For example, there was a change from a Permanent Indian Frontier, to a policy of concentration on large reservations, to Grant's Peace Policy and small reservations. Indigenous nations in the USA were frequently forced to move from one location to another. We also can agree that US policy towards Indigenous nations was not just: it was not fair to agree a treaty and then fail to meet treaty obligations by not paying annuities or protecting Indigenous land from settlers. The point about immigration is interesting: if the USA had not expanded so fast, perhaps the 'Indian problem' would not have occurred as it did.

  While Interpretation A provides an accurate account of challenges facing Indigenous people, the conclusion the author reaches about the inevitable consequences of this approach to dealing with the 'Indian problem' is not convincing. Unlike Interpretation B, which describes a policy where Indigenous people are not compelled to assimilate into US society, Interpretation A sees it as inevitable that Indigenous people will have to be made 'extinct'.

Page 49
INTERPRETATION ANALYSIS

a 1 'Sometimes my young men would attack the Indians who were our enemies and took their ponies. They did it in return.'

  2 'We had bison for food, and their hides for clothing and for our tipis.'

  3 'We preferred hunting to a life of idleness on the reservation, where we were driven against our will.'

  4 'At times we did not get enough to eat and we were not allowed to leave the reservation to hunt.'

  5 'We preferred our own way of living. We were no expense to the government when we lived that way.'

b Your answer might conclude that the content of the interpretation is convincing, because there is a lot of evidence, including from President Grant's own evaluation of the need for a new peace policy in 1869, that reservations were leaving Indigenous people facing a choice between resistance and starvation. However, we also know that Custer ordered an immediate attack on Sitting Bull's village or camp, without any attempt to reach a diplomatic solution or allow non-combatants (women, children, the elderly) to leave the battlefield, and there had been many other occasions (such as Sand Creek) where US military forces had massacred women, children and old people. As a result, Interpretation A is convincing on long-term reasons why the Lakota and Cheyenne fought the Battle of the Little Big Horn, but it does not discuss the specific events leading up to the battle.

DESCRIBE

a
- Treaties: The US government did not stick to the promises it made when it signed treaties. For example, in order to build the first transcontinental railroad, new treaties were signed that 'extinguished' previously agreed Indigenous rights to the land. The Fort Laramie Treaty of 1868 was also broken when gold was discovered in Paha Sapa (Black Hills) in 1874.
- Gold: Following the discovery of gold in Paha Sapa (Black Hills) in 1874, the US government first tried to buy the area from the Lakota for $6 million in 1875. When Lakota leaders refused the offer, the US government declared that all bands must return to their reservations or be treated as 'hostile'.
- Railroads: When Indigenous people resisted being moved away from railroad routes, they were attacked following instructions from the US government.
- Military campaigns: Sherman's troops destroyed Indigenous crops, killed their horses, burned their camps during winter, and destroyed all their hunting weapons to protect transcontinental railroad workers. Then, in early 1876, troops were sent after bands that did not return to their reservations following the discovery of gold in Paha Sapa (Black Hills) in 1874.
- Bison: When Indigenous nations resisted the transcontinental railroads, the US Army destroyed bison herds. It even encouraged Euro-Americans to visit the Plains to kill as many bison as possible. This forced the Lakota and Cheyenne to decide between starvation or reservations.
- Reservations: Corrupt Indian agents held back annuities or provided poor-quality food rations and goods. Later, food rations were reduced to force nations into farming. The US government insisted on Lakota and Cheyenne bands returning to reservations in 1875, in an attempt to prevent them resisting the gold rush in Paha Sapa (Black Hills).

b Use two problems from the list above to describe two problems in detail.

Page 51
INTERPRETATION ANALYSIS

a 27 years

b Military campaigns that attacked villages and camps, destroying stores and capturing or killing horses so that Indigenous bands had no resources left; carrying out these campaigns in winter so that the Indigenous bands had no way to replace their lost resources and faced starvation; forcing bands onto reservations where they could be kept under strict control by Indian agents and the military (stationed in forts nearby); exterminating the bison so that Indigenous horse nations no longer had any way to live independently; once Indigenous nations were dependent on the government for food, holding back food supplies if people on reservations did not follow the rules; reducing the size of reservations so hunting was no longer possible as a way of feeding people.

c The Lakota and Cheyenne

d People who are dependent on the government for food

e It has a positive opinion of the response. It says that the USA 'rose high above defeat', which means that it was not crushed by defeat but instead showed its superiority, first using military power (this was 'soon accomplished') and then by settling the lands of the Lakota and Cheyenne and reducing these nations to 'hopeless wards', dependent on the US government for food.

IN WHAT WAYS

a
- The Fort Laramie Treaty of 1851 set out the boundaries of Lakota territory, which included Paha Sapa (Black Hills). The US government agreed to pay the eight nations that signed the treaty an annuity of $50,000 for 50 years (later reduced to ten years), in money for the first five years and then in goods. However, the government did nothing to stop migrants settling on Indigenous lands. Many Indigenous bands decided they had no other choice but to fight back. The conflicts that followed between 1862 and 1868 were, at the time, called the 'Indian Wars'.
- The Fort Laramie Treaty of 1868 followed Red Cloud's victory against the USA. The Great Sioux Reservation (an area of 48,000 square miles) was guaranteed for the Oceti Sakowin forever. The treaty also said that no non-Indigenous person, apart from US government officials, 'shall ever be permitted to pass over, settle upon, or reside' in the Great Sioux Reservation, which included the sacred Paha Sapa (Black Hills). However, the treaty did not stop Custer's expedition into the Black Hills, or stop the gold rush that followed. The refusal by Lakota bands to allow the gold rush to happen led to a military campaign against them. This in turn led to the Battle of the Little Big Horn in 1876, where the US Army was defeated.
- The Act of 1877 overturned the Fort Laramie Treaty of 1868. It took the Black Hills (Paha Sapa) away from the Lakota and broke up the rest of the Great Sioux Reservation into smaller reservations. It said that the US government was now allowed to build roads across Lakota land, and a large area of the original reservation was opened up for non-Indigenous settlement.

b The Fort Laramie Treaty of 1851, the Fort Laramie Treaty of 1868 and the Act of 1877 can be used to demonstrate how US government policy towards Indigenous people changed. A good answer will use the information from the bullet points above to consider the different ways the lives of Indigenous people were affected by these changes in policy. The discussion will be supported by detailed information throughout.

Page 53
INTERPRETATION ANALYSIS

a Euro-Americans/citizens of the USA

b Indigenous nations such as the Lakota believed that everything, including land, was created by the Great Spirit, *Wakan Tanka*, for people to use. People should protect and care for the land entrusted to their nation, but land couldn't belong to anyone. This fits with Interpretation B. Sitting Bull calls the earth 'this mother of ours', and criticises the way Euro-Americans claim the Earth for their own use, put up fences so the land can't be shared, and make it ugly by putting up buildings and leaving rubbish. He criticises the way Euro-Americans overuse the soil and then use medicine (fertilisers) to make it produce crops again.

c 'Tribal Indians' might refer to the way Indigenous nations lived communally rather than as individuals. The Dawes Act of 1887 aimed to break up this communal way of life, and undermine the power of chiefs.

d 1 Interpretation B is opposed to Euro-American ideas about how the land should be used, saying that Euro-Americans 'fence their neighbours away from [the Earth], and deface [the Earth] with their buildings and their refuse'. Interpretation A, on the other hand, says that adopting Euro-American ways of using land would be good for Indigenous people because they would have 'secure' food supplies and wouldn't have to listen to 'what the chief or any one else says'.

2 Interpretation B is the reported speech of Sitting Bull, who went to war to oppose the Euro-American colonisation of Indigenous land. Interpretation A was written by a US military officer who spent part of his career fighting Indigenous people to prevent them resisting Euro-American colonisation.

3 Interpretation B is convincing because Sitting Bull's words are supported by what we know about Lakota beliefs about the land. Your answer to part b above will help you argue this point.

You could argue that Interpretation A is less convincing because, although Crook's opinion matches the aims of the Dawes Act of 1887 (which wanted to break up the communal way of life of Indigenous people and destroy the power of chiefs), the consequences for most Indigenous people were not positive. Once the 25-year period was up, many Indigenous people sold their 'little farms' because they could not afford to start paying taxes on them.

However, you could also argue Interpretation A is convincing because Crook is saying that destroying the influence of chiefs will reduce armed resistance against the USA. This was the result of the Dawes Act, in combination with brutal military suppression of the Indigenous nations of the Plains.

You could conclude that Interpretation B is more convincing because it is accurate, and because Interpretation A applies Euro-American ideas about land to Indigenous people and the positive predictions in Interpretation A did not come true.

Page 55

INTERPRETATION ANALYSIS

a Hunger

b A belief that the Messiah will destroy all the Euro-American settlers and bring the bison herds back to the Plains in huge numbers.

c Some Indigenous leaders, such as Sitting Bull, exploited the Ghost Dance movement to get back their power. However, General Miles saw what they were up to and was able to prevent the unrest spreading outside reservations.

d Hunger was certainly a reason why Indigenous nations longed for all Euro-American colonisation to be swept from the Plains and for the bison to return, but Interpretation A is not convincing when it says that the cause of the Ghost Dance was that Indigenous nations simply wanted their 'preferred food' back again. They wanted much more than this; they wanted their land and their ways of life returned to them. Also, the Ghost Dance was more about communities dancing together to bring the past back, than about people waiting for a 'Messiah' to deliver them from the USA. Furthermore, Miles's description of the consequences of the Ghost Dance are not convincing. He does not mention that the US mistakenly believed the Ghost Dance was a war dance, and does not acknowledge that this mistake led directly to the death of Sitting Bull, and also to the Wounded Knee Massacre.

BULLET POINTS

a You could base your diagram on the information about conditions on reservations on page 54 of this Revision Guide, and add in other information that you know.

b A good answer will explain that railroads were an important reason for the extermination of the bison. The US Army guarded railroad workers, attacked Indigenous communities and destroyed bison herds. It even encouraged Euro-Americans to visit the Plains to kill as many bison as possible.

A good answer will then consider government actions as the more important reason. The great bison herds were systematically exterminated as part of President Grant's Peace Policy. The US government wanted to force Indigenous people to farm and one way it did this was by instructing the US Army to reduce bison numbers so that horse nations would have to stay in one place and grow food.

A good answer will end with a conclusion that states and justifies which reason was more important. There is no right or wrong answer, but the choice needs to be justified. For example, you could argue that the railroads encouraged hunting but it was the US government's intention to exterminate the bison herds that was the most important reason for their extermination. The railroads meant the extermination of the bison happened sooner than it would have done if they had not been constructed across the Plains, but it would have happened eventually given US government policy.

Page 57

IN WHAT WAYS

a • The Indian Removal Act of 1830 and Indian Territory: The Indian Removal Act of 1830 permitted the US government to make treaties with Indigenous nations to swap Indigenous land in the East for land in 'Indian Territory'. More than 125,000 Indigenous people were forced to leave their homes between 1830 and 1850. Thousands died on the 'Trail of Tears' to 'Indian Territory', including 4,000 Cherokee. Euro-Americans rushed in to grab the land Indigenous people were made to leave.

• The Oregon Trail: The US government wanted US citizens to move to the new territories in the Far West, but the journey by sea was long and expensive. Getting there by land would be quicker and cheaper, but migrants needed a route through the Rocky Mountains. The establishment of the Oregon Trail – a reliable 2,000 miles overland route from the Missouri River to Oregon City – solved the problem and the trail was key to early settlement of the West. By 1869 (when the first transcontinental railroad was completed), more than 400,000 people had migrated to the Far West along the Oregon Trail.

• The Mormon migration to the Great Salt Lake Valley: By 1870, over 70,000 Mormons had migrated to the Great Salt Lake Valley, following the route carefully planned by Brigham Young and the Pioneer Band.

• The California Gold Rush: In 1849, around 90,000 people arrived in California to prospect for gold. By 1855, the population of California had increased to 300,000. Two-thirds of migrants were from the USA, the rest were from countries all round the world, including China. The rapid increase in population meant California became a US state in 1850. Indigenous people suffered greatly as a result of violence by miners, diseases spread by the new arrivals and thefts of their land. The Indigenous population of California was 100,000 before the Gold Rush; by 1870 it was 30,000.

• The Fort Laramie Treaty of 1851 and the Fort Laramie Treaty of 1868: The Fort Laramie Treaty of 1851 provided safe passage for overland migrants through Indigenous lands in return for annuity payments and government protection from 'depredation'. The Indigenous nations that signed the treaty soon found that migrant settlers had very little respect for their rights, and the US government rarely acted to prevent them breaking the terms of the treaty. The Fort Laramie Treaty of 1868 followed the USA's defeat in Red Cloud's War. Under the treaty, no one apart from Indigenous people and authorised government officials were permitted to enter the Great Sioux Reservation. It was a block to settlement that lasted until the discovery of gold on sacred land in the Black Hills (Paha Sapa) in 1874.

• The completion of the first transcontinental railroad in 1869: This opened up the Plains for settlement in two ways. The railroad companies were incentivised by the Pacific Railroad Act of 1872 to sell the land they had been given by the US government and, by 1880, they had sold 200 million acres in the West for settlement. Secondly, people wanted to settle near the railroad because of the advantages it offered; for example, farmers could send crops to markets in the East and the Far West by rail, and order new machinery from the East to tackle the problems of farming the Plains.

• Reservations: To settle the Plains, the US government made treaties with Indigenous nations, persuading them to give up their homelands in return for reservations and annuities. Non-Indigenous settlers were banned from reservations to prevent conflict, but the US government had not stopped Euro-Americans settling on areas of reservation land and Indigenous people often left their reservations to hunt or raid. The perceived need for more land for Euro-American settlement, the desire to reduce conflict between Indigenous and non-Indigenous groups of people, and the idea that Indigenous people should support themselves by farming, all led to a policy of small reservations and reduced support for Indigenous people from the US government.

b A good answer will use the information from the table to consider the different ways the expansion of the USA affected the lives of different groups of people. The discussion will be supported by detailed information about each group.

Glossary

A

abolitionist: someone who campaigned for the abolition of slavery

assimilate: adopt the customs, language and culture of a more powerful group or society

B

band: a group of Indigenous people who share a common language, culture or territory; bands are often linked by family relationships

bison: a large, shaggy-haired animal; used to be called buffalo, but is not related to buffalo found in other countries and is now referred to more accurately as bison

C

carpetbagger: an insult used by southerners to describe northerners who moved to the South after the American Civil War to take advantage of economic opportunities

Confederacy: the government formed by the southern states that seceded from the USA between 1861 and 1865 during the American Civil War

Congress: the part of the US government that creates and passes laws

council: a group of people who meet to discuss and make decisions

counting coup: an Indigenous practice of touching an enemy in battle and escaping unharmed

E

Emancipation: the act of setting a person or a group of people free from slavery

Euro-Americans: people of European heritage who settled in North America

F

federal government: the government of the USA; it is in charge of things that affect the whole country

freedpeople: formerly enslaved people who were granted freedom by Emancipation in 1863; also referred to as emancipated people

H

hide: the skin of an animal, particularly when it has been removed and treated for use in clothing or other goods

homesteaders: settlers who established small family farms on land granted to them by the US government

horse nations: Indigenous nations that relied heavily on horses for transportation and hunting

I

Indian agents: US government officials who were responsible for managing relations with Indigenous nations and carrying out federal policies related to Indigenous peoples

Indigenous people: the original inhabitants of a particular country or region

industrialisation: the process of developing large-scale industries and manufacturing

inflation: an increase in the prices of goods and services over time

M

Manifest Destiny: the belief that God gave the USA a mission to expand its territory, culture and values to all of America

martial law: imposing military control in times of emergency or unrest

militia: a group of citizens organised for military service in times of emergency or defence

Mormons: members of the Church of Jesus Christ of Latter-day Saints; a religious group

N

nation: a group of people who share a common language, culture or identity

nomadic: a way of life where individuals and groups move from place to place

O

Oceti Sakowin: the 'Seven Council Fires' brought together seven nations, including the Lakota; non-Indigenous people sometimes called the Oceti Sakowin a disrespectful name, the 'Great Sioux Nation'

P

plantation: an enormous farm used to grow crops such as cotton and tobacco; in the USA enslaved people were forced to do the work on plantations until the end of the Civil War

R

Radical Republicans: a political group that dominated Congress and wanted strict Reconstruction policies in the southern states and the protection of civil rights after the Civil War

Reconstruction: the period after the Civil War in which the USA sought to rebuild and re-establish the southern states

reservations: areas of land set aside by the US government for Indigenous nations; often a much smaller area than a nation's original homelands, the rest of which were opened up for settlement by non-Indigenous people

S

secede: to withdraw from a larger group or organisation; used to refer to the southern states withdrawing from the United States in the lead-up to the Civil War

sod: a thick layer of soil and grass held together by tangled roots

sovereign nations: groups of people living in the same place who govern themselves and have the power to make their own decisions

T

tariffs: taxes or duties put on imported or exported goods

tipi: a dwelling in the shape of a cone and made out of animal hides, used by some Indigenous nations

U

unorganised territory: a region that is not part of any organised governmental structure; often used to describe western areas of America that were not incorporated into official territories or states

V

veterans: people who have been in the armed forces

W

wards: members of Indigenous nations placed under the legal guardianship of the US government, often as part of efforts to assimilate or 'civilise' them; by using the term 'wards', the US government saw itself as the 'guardian' of Indigenous nations

warrior societies: military units in Indigenous societies

white supremacist: a person or group that holds racist beliefs about the superiority of white people and seeks to establish and maintain systems of racial inequality and oppression

Topics available from *Oxford AQA GCSE History*

Student Books

Paper 1: Understanding the modern world

Period studies

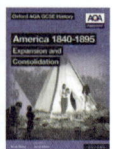
America 1840–1895 Expansion and Consolidation Student Book
978 138 204407 3

Germany 1890–1945 Democracy and Dictatorship Student Book
978 019 837010 9

America 1920–1973 Opportunity and Inequality Student Book
978 019 841262 5

Wider world depth studies

Conflict and Tension: First World War 1894–1918 Student Book
978 019 842900 5

Conflict and Tension: The Inter-War Years 1918–1939 Student Book
978 019 837011 6

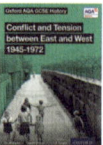
Conflict and Tension between East and West 1945–1972 Student Book
978 019 841266 3

Conflict and Tension in Asia 1950–1975 Student Book
978 019 841264 9

Paper 2: Shaping the nation

Thematic studies

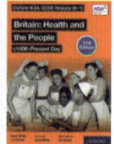
Britain: Health and the People c1000–Present Day Second Edition Student Book
978 138 202310 8

Britain: Power and the People c1170–Present Day Second Edition Student Book
978 138 202313 9

Britain: Migration, Empires and the People c790–Present Day Second Edition Student Book
978 138 202307 8

British depth studies

British Depth Studies c1066–1685 Second Edition Student Book
978 138 204512 4

Above includes all four Depth Study options: Norman, Medieval, Elizabethan and Restoration England

Norman England c1066–c1100 Second Edition Student Book
978 138 204518 6

Elizabethan England c1568–1603 Second Edition Student Book
978 138 204515 5

Covering all 16 AQA options

Teacher Handbook
978 019 837018 5

Kerboodle Exam Practice and Revision
978 019 837019 2

Access digital versions of the Student Books on

Revision Guides

Paper 1: Understanding the modern world

Period studies

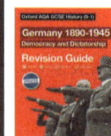
America 1840–1895 Expansion and Consolidation Revision Guide
978 138 204405 9

Germany 1890–1945 Democracy and Dictatorship Revision Guide
978 019 842289 1

America 1920–1973 Opportunity and Inequality Revision Guide
978 019 843282 1

Wider world depth studies

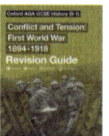
Conflict and Tension: First World War 1894–1918 Revision Guide
978 138 200767 2

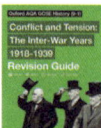
Conflict and Tension: The Inter-War Years 1918–1939 Revision Guide
978 019 842291 4

Conflict and Tension between East and West 1945–1972 Revision Guide
978 019 843288 3

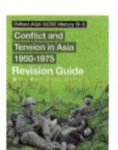
Conflict and Tension in Asia 1950–1975 Revision Guide
978 019 843286 9

Paper 2: Shaping the nation

Thematic studies

Britain: Health and the People c1000–Present Day Revision Guide
978 019 842295 2

Britain: Power and the People c1170–Present Day Revision Guide
978 019 843290 6

Britain: Migration, Empires and the People c790–Present Day Revision Guide
978 138 201503 5

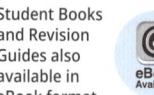
Student Books and Revision Guides also available in eBook format

British depth studies

Norman England c1066–c1100 Revision Guide
978 019 843284 5

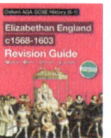
Elizabethan England c1568–1603 Revision Guide
978 019 842293 8

Scan the QR code to find out more and order – or visit **www.oxfordsecondary.com/aqa-gcse-history**